ECONOMIC HISTORY

THE PORTUGAL TRADE

INTERNATIONAL TRADE

THE PORTUGAL TRADE

A study of Anglo-Portugeuse commerce 1700–1770

H.E.S. FISHER

Routledge
Taylor & Francis Group
LONDON AND NEW YORK

First published in 1971 by
Routledge
2 Park Square, Milton Park, Abingdon, Oxfordshire, OX14 4RN
711 Third Avenue, New York, NY 10017

First issued in paperback 2014

Routledge is an imprint of the Taylor & Francis Group, an informa business

British Library Cataloguing in Publication Data
A CIP catalogue record for this book
is available from the British Library

The Portugal Trade
ISBN 0-415-37979-2 (volume)
ISBN 0-415-37978-4 (subset)
ISBN 0-415-28619-0 (set)

ISBN 978-1-138-86500-6 (pbk)
ISBN 978-0-415-37979-3 (hbk)

Routledge Library Editions: Economic History

THE PORTUGAL TRADE

The Custom House, London, 1714

THE PORTUGAL TRADE

A Study of Anglo-Portuguese Commerce 1700-1770

H. E. S. Fisher

Methuen & Co Ltd
LONDON

First published in 1971
by Methuen & Co. Ltd
11 New Fetter Lane, London EC4

SBN 416 17650 X

Distributed in the USA by
Barnes & Noble Inc.

To my parents

Contents

Acknowledgements

IN PREPARING THIS STUDY, first as a doctoral thesis for the Faculty of Economics of the University of London, and then, in a considerably revised form, for publication, I have received help from many quarters. I should like to express my gratitude to the Trustees of the Eileen Power Memorial Fund and to the Scholarships Committee of the University of London who generously financed my two years of full-time research, and to the latter's Central Research Fund who helped meet the cost of a research visit to Portugal. The staffs of the archives and libraries I worked in were invariably most willing to assist and to guide. I am particularly indebted, in England, to the staff of the Public Record Office, the British Museum, the libraries of the Universities of London, Cambridge and Exeter, the libraries of H.M. Customs and the Stock Exchange, London, and the Corporation of London Record Office; and, in Portugal, to the staff of the Arquivo Torre de Tombo and the Biblioteca Nacional, Lisbon. I am grateful to the following individuals and institutions who very kindly gave me permission to examine private collections of records: to the Marquess of Cholmondeley for permission to examine the Cholmondeley (Houghton) MSS. at Cambridge; to Dr José Pereira de Lima for allowing me to examine the Hunt, Roope business records in Vila Nova; to Mr P. C. Kendall for allowing me to see the Offley, Forrester records in Vila Nova; to Dr P. Alvares Ribeiro for permission to examine records belonging to the Real Companhia dos Vinhos do Porto; to the Bank of England for permission to examine certain of its records, and to Mr L. de Rouet of Offley, Forrester, London, for enabling me to see Robert Wilmot's ledger. I am grateful too to Miss M. E. Turner, Dr E. F. J. Mathews, Dr K. H. Burley and Dr J. K. Edwards for permission to consult and draw on their unpublished theses. My understanding of the subject and of the sources for its study benefited from conversations with many people. In this respect I should especially like to record my thanks to Professor C. R. Boxer for his good counsel at the outset of my studies, and to Professor Virgínia Rau, Dr Jorge de Macedo, Sir Ralph Newman, Señor F. da Silva Teixeira and Dr Carlos Estorninho. I am very appreciative of the help rendered by colleagues at Exeter, Dr F. R. Oliver for advice on statistical matters, Mrs P. Castle for help with some of the statistical calculations, Mr R. E. J. Fry for drawing the graphs, and, above all, Mr B. W. Clapp and Professor W. E. Minchinton for their careful reading of my drafts and their many useful suggestions. I am grateful too to Mrs P. Toynbee and Miss M. Makepeace, who were mainly responsible for the typing of the various manuscripts. I wish also to thank the Editors of the *Economic History Review* for permission to incorporate as part of Chapters 1 and 2 an article published in their pages. My greatest debt, however, is owed to Professor A. H. John, under whom the work was begun, and who has been constant in helpful criticism and encouragement.

Exeter, December 1969.

Plates

ACKNOWLEDGEMENTS

The author and publishers wish to thank the following for permission to reproduce the illustrations listed below:

The Trustees of the British Museum for plates 1, 7, 9 and 11

Casa de Portugal for plate 5

The Controller of H.M. Stationery Office for plate 2, from Crown-copyright records in the Public Record Office

Mr and Mrs Paul Mellon for plate 10, portrait of *Arthur Holdsworth, Thomas Taylor and Captain Stancombe*, by Arthur Devis

The National Portrait Gallery for plate 3, a detail from the portrait, *John, Duke of Montague and Lord Tyrawly*

The Post Office for plate 8

The Science Museum for the frontispiece

The Victoria and Albert Museum for plate 4

The contemporary model of an 80-gun English warship (plate 6) was lent to the Science Museum, London, by the late Mrs J. O. Humphry.

Cover illustration, The National Maritime Museum:
Lisbon, 1702 (engraving by Schenk)

Text Figures

Abbreviations

A.H.R.	*American Historical Review*
Annales	*Annales, Économies, Sociétés, Civilisations*
B.M.	British Museum
B.N.	Biblioteca Nacional, Lisbon
B. of E.	Bank of England
Cal. H. of L. MSS.	*Calendar of House of Lords MSS.*
Cal. S.P. Col. (A.W.I.)	*Calendar of State Papers, Colonial Series. America and West Indies*
Cal. Treas. Books	*Calendar of Treasury Books*
Chol. (H.) MSS.	Cholmondeley (Houghton) MSS.
C.M.E.	Chancery Masters' Exhibits
Col. Pomb.	Colecção Pombalina
Ec.H.R.	*Economic History Review*
F.F.	Arquivo dos Feitos Findos
F.G.	Fundo Geral
H.A.H.R.	*Hispanic American Historical Review*
H.R. (V.N.).	Hunt, Roope and Company Library, Vila Nova de Gaia
J. do C.	Junta do Comercio
J.Ec.H.	*Journal of Economic History*
Journal of Trade	*Journal of the Commissioners for Trade and Plantations*
M. dos N.E.	Ministerio dos Negocios Estrangeiros
O.F. (Lond.)	Offley, Forrester and Company, London
O.F. (V.N.).	Offley, Forrester and Company, Vila Nova de Gaia
P.R.O.	Public Record Office
R.C.V.P.	Real Companhia dos Vinhos do Porto
Rev. de H.	*Revista de Historia*

Introduction

HISTORIANS HAVE LONG drawn attention to the expansion of English foreign trade in the seventeenth and eighteenth centuries as a prime cause of the Industrial Revolution in England. And in considering the reasons underlying the growth of English trade, they have, for the period from the mid-seventeenth century onwards, given great emphasis to the developing connections with the English colonies and trading centres outside Europe. In an age when industrial self-sufficiency was increasing in most European countries, and when no major change occurred in either the pattern or costs of English industrial output or in transport costs, it is clear that extra-European interests had great significance for trade expansion. The development of production in English America and Asia of goods with an expansive English and European demand (sugar, tobacco and tea in particular) not only sustained a remarkable growth of imports into England but an expansion of re-exports to the Continent. From these developments, too, stemmed the effective demand for an expanding flow of English manufactures to the non-European areas.

In two papers published in recent years Professor Davis has added much to our knowledge of this process.[1] Using the official English trade figures, he has indicated that from a low level in about 1640 English trade with the English non-European areas thereafter expanded impressively (although not steadily) down to the early 1770s, and that this secular expansion constituted the principal dynamic element in the general growth of English foreign trade. The following table, based on the figures presented in Davis's articles, summarizes the position.

[1] Ralph Davis, 'English Foreign Trade, 1660-1700', *Ec.H.R.*, 2nd series, Vol. VII (1954); and 'English Foreign Trade, 1700-1774', *Ec.H.R.*, 2nd series, Vol. XV (1962).

Table I

	Total Imports into England (£ million annual average)	*Percentage of Total Imports coming from English America, Africa and Asia*	*Total Exports from England (£ million annual average)*	*Percentage of Total Exports going to the English non-European areas, together with re-exports of American or Asian goods*
1662-3/1668-9	4·4	—	4·1	—
1699-1701	5·8	32	6·4	34
1752-4	8·2	46	11·9	44
1772-4	12·7	53	15·7	62

Note: Asia covers the area traded to by the East India Company. The figures for the English non-European areas include the very minor trade recorded to and from Spanish America. The 1662-3/1668-9 figures refer to two single years running from Michaelmas to Michaelmas respectively.

Stress has been placed above on the *English* commercial interests outside Europe. This conforms with the approach generally followed by historians writing on the English 'Commercial Revolution' who have seen the expansion of English commerce very much as a process related to English extra-European interests alone. America's role, however, was greater than that of the English colonies. For the usual approach fails to take into account the part played by the Spanish and Portuguese colonies in America. This neglect is partly explained by the great reliance which, naturally enough, has been placed on the official English trade statistics, especially the annual series from 1697 produced by the Inspectors-General of the Customs, P.R.O. Customs 3. Drawn up as they are on the basis of direct trade with foreign countries, these figures show virtually no trade with the Iberian empires in America and naturally fail to reveal the importance of these empires for English trade with Spain and Portugal themselves. The effect has been that the role of colonial America as a whole in English commercial growth has not been appreciated to the full, while that of Europe and of English America and Asia has been somewhat overstated.

Although no overall study has been made of Spanish America's contribution to English commercial growth, it is possible to indicate the main outlines of this contribution from the studies that have been made of Spanish and Anglo-Spanish commerce. First of all, the growth of English exports to Spain itself depended to some extent on Spanish-American factors. Official exports to Spain grew little between 1660 and the end of the century – London's shipments alone averaged £448,000 annually in 1662-3 and 1668-9,[1] while in 1699-1701 total English exports averaged £539,000 annually.[2] But between 1700 and the mid-1760s total exports roughly doubled to over £1 million annually, although the expansion was by no means smooth.[3] Throughout the period from the mid-seventeenth century the manufactures sent to Spain, the bulk of all exports, were in part re-exported to Spanish America.[4] Such transhipments of manufactures owed their existence basically to the relative economic backwardness of the Spanish colonies, with agriculture and mining very much the dominant activities. They stemmed too from Spain's orthodox imperial economic policies which restricted the development of colonial manufacturing and aimed at confining colonial trade to Spanish ports and Spanish nationals. Spain's inability to sustain her role fully in this system, because of her poorly developed domestic industries and her relatively limited mercantile capital, led her merchants to turn towards the manufactures and generous credit of Northern Europe.[5]

How far the growth of English exports to Spain sprang from metropolitan or colonial demands cannot be answered from the existing

[1] B.M. Add. MSS. 36,785. The years ran from Michaelmas to Michaelmas. Shipments would also have been made from the outports.

[2] C. Whitworth, *State of the Trade of Great Britain* (1776), Part II, p. 31.

[3] Shipments fell greatly during the War of the Spanish Succession but thereafter grew, reaching the pre-war level by 1720 and averaging £990,000 annually by 1736-8. They again slumped during the war of 1739-48, but recovered with the return of peace, usually exceeding £1 million annually until 1769, when they began to decline. Ibid., pp. 31-2, and D. MacPherson, *Annals of Commerce* (1805), Vol. III, *passim*. In both the wars of 1702-13 and 1739-48 English goods were introduced into Spain by other means. See, respectively, Chapter 1, pp. 38-9, and R. Pares, *War and Trade in the West Indies, 1739-1763* (Oxford, 1936), pp. 124-5. These figures can be taken as broadly indicating the actual movements in the trade, the considerations applying to the figures of the Portugal trade noted in Chapter 1, p. 13n., generally applying here as well.

[4] J. O. McLachlan, *Trade and Peace with Old Spain, 1667-1750* (Cambridge, 1940), pp. 11-15, 37, 64; A. Christelow, 'Great Britain and the Trades from Cadiz and Lisbon to Spanish America and Brazil, 1759-1783', *H.A.H.R.*, Vol. XXVII (1947), pp. 2-4, 17-18.

[5] On Spanish colonial policy, and the state of industry and trade in Spain and her colonies, see, *inter alia*, C. H. Haring, *Trade and Navigation between Spain and the Indies in the Time of the Hapsburgs* (Cambridge, Mass., 1918), and *The Spanish Empire in America* (New York, 1947); J. O. McLachlan, op. cit.; and R. Herr, *The Eighteenth Century Revolution in Spain* (Princeton, 1958).

studies. But it is likely that colonial demands did grow. Mexico, the richest and most populous province, roughly doubled its silver output between 1701-20 and 1761-80 from an average of 163,800 kg annually to 366,400 kg.[1] With other evidence of growing prosperity,[2] this suggests some growth of Mexican demand for English manufactures, and demand may well have risen elsewhere in Spanish America. Moreover, the increasing flow of American revenues and profits to the Crown and the mercantile classes in Spain, given their income-generating effect, must have stimulated the metropolitan market for English manufactures.[3] As the increase in English exports of manufactures to Spain between 1700 and 1750 amounted to about one-eighth of the total increase in English exports of manufactures, the Spanish market's buoyancy was by no means insignificant.

Spanish America had little bearing on the officially recorded import trade from Spain into England, only certain minor imports such as indigo and cochineal coming originally from across the Atlantic. But during the period large quantities of American silver bullion entered England from Spain, unrecorded by the Customs, as the principal means of settlement of Spain's trading deficits with England.[4] The English figures show that from 1697 until 1711 England usually had a visible trade deficit with Spain, but that thereafter to 1770, except for three years, she achieved a surplus: from 1712 to 1730 it averaged £150,000 annually, from 1731 to 1738, £350,000, and after falling in the 1740s averaged £660,000 between 1749 and 1770.[5] These surpluses can be taken to indicate broadly the actual surpluses on current account, as the considerations applying to the Anglo-Portuguese trade account reviewed below essentially also apply to Anglo-Spanish trade.[6] This being so, such silver shipments to England between 1712

[1] A. Soetbeer, *Edelmetall-Produktion und Werthverhältnis zwischen Gold und Silber* (Gotha, 1879), p. 60 et seq.

[2] See C. H. Haring, *The Spanish Empire in America*, pp. 269, 304-5.

[3] For the increasing royal receipts from America, see ibid., pp. 275, 304-5. The decline in English exports to Spain after 1769 was probably due to Charles III's policy of encouraging home industries and restricting imports of foreign manufactures. See R. Herr, op. cit., Chapter V.

[4] J. O. McLachlan, op. cit., pp. 13-14; A. Christelow, op. cit., pp. 6-7, 19-20; V. L. Brown, 'Anglo-French Rivalry for the Trade of the Spanish Peninsula, 1763-1783', *Smith College Studies in History*, Vol. XV (1929-30), pp. 53-7.

[5] C. Whitworth, op. cit., Part II, pp. 31-2.

[6] Chapter 1, pp. 19-20, Chapter 2, p. 43. The considerations include the existence of English 'invisible' earnings in Spain, notably from shipments of Newfoundland cod, which help offset the exaggeration of the official surpluses to 1750.

and 1770 may have totalled some £14 million, the equivalent of about 3 per cent of all recorded English imports.

English commerce also benefited from more direct trades with Spanish-America. Throughout the period, some of the goods declared for the English Caribbean islands were sold to Spanish colonists.[1] This business was fostered by their growing demands, the favourable position of Jamaica for such traffic, and the inefficiency and corruption of the Spanish Customs service. Measurement is out of the question, but such dealings clearly stimulated the growth of exports to Jamaica, which rose from £114,000 annually in 1699-1701 to £400-£500,000 annually in the 1760s.[2] In addition, between 1713 and 1739 such trade was supplemented by the South Sea Company's 'annual ship' concession for trade with Spanish America, and by the Company's and its employees' contraband business.[3] Probably the goods involved were mostly included among shipments recorded for the Spanish West Indies (usually these were very small but for seven of the years between 1713 and 1739 they were between £150-£250,000)[4] but undoubtedly some had been declared for English possessions. From 1660 to 1770, too, many thousands of African negroes were sold to the Spanish colonists by Englishmen, by private traders, by the successive African Companies, and by the South Sea Company under the Asiento.[5] The Spanish colonists paid for these imports in dyestuffs and drugs but mainly in silver, all being remitted usually to England, along with more silver shipped on the account of Spaniards, merchants and others, who wished to avoid the dues on silver sent to Spain. Silver was also sold by Spanish colonists for

[1] C. H. Haring, *Trade and Navigation between Spain and the Indies*, pp. 120-1; C. Nettels, 'England and the Spanish American Trade, 1680-1715', *Journal of Modern History*, Vol. III (1931), *passim*; V. L. Brown, 'Anglo-Spanish Relations in America in the Closing Years of the Colonial Era', *H.A.H.R.*, Vol. V (1922), pp. 374-82, and 'Contraband Trade: A Factor in the Decline of Spain's Empire in America', *H.A.H.R.*, Vol. III (1928), *passim*; R. Pares, op. cit., *passim*; A. Christelow, 'Contraband Trade between Jamaica and the Spanish Main, and the Free Port Act of 1766', *H.A.H.R.*, Vol. XXII (1942), *passim*.

[2] C. Whitworth, op. cit., Part II, pp. 57-8.

[3] J. O. McLachlan, op. cit., *passim*; V. L. Brown, 'The South Sea Company and Contraband Trade', *A.H.R.*, Vol. XXXI (1926), *passim*; G. H. Nelson, 'Contraband Trade under the Asiento, 1730-1739', *A.H.R.*, Vol. LI (1945), *passim*.

[4] C. Whitworth, op. cit., Part II, p. 80.

[5] C. Nettels, op. cit., *passim*; J. O. McLachlan, op. cit., *passim*; V. L. Brown, *H.A.H.R.*, Vol. VIII (1928), *passim*; R. Pares, op. cit., *passim*; K. G. Davies, *The Royal African Company* (1957), pp. 326-35.

bills of exchange drawn on London; presumably, too, it was mostly shipped to England.[1]

English manufactures also went to Spanish America via England's trade with Portugal. Between 1713 and 1762 considerable quantities were shipped from Lisbon and Oporto to Brazil, from there to Buenos Aires, and thence to Chile and Peru.[2] Payment was largely made in silver, swelling the unrecorded bullion remittances from Portugal to England during this period. Noteworthy too were the small trades in provisions conducted by the New England and Jamaica merchants with the Spanish colonists.[3] These trades undoubtedly grew from their mid-seventeenth-century levels and, small as they were, by increasing the English colonies' incomes and money supply marginally enhanced their ability to import from England.

Together, then, the Spanish American empire contributed to English commercial growth by providing an additional market for English manufactures in America, by sustaining metropolitan Spanish demands for English manufactures, by supplying by no means inconsiderable quantities of silver, and by the opportunities it gave to English and colonial-English merchants to supplement their incomes through the slave and North American foodstuff trades.

The contribution of Brazil to the English 'Commercial Revolution' has also been neglected by historians. This neglect stems not only from the English trade statistics which show no trade with Brazil and fail to reveal the importance of Luso-Brazilian trade for English trade with Portugal; but also from the slight indications of its importance to be found in the sole general study so far made of Anglo-Portuguese trade in the century after 1660, which is to be found in V. M. Shillington and A. B. W. Chapman's *The Commercial Relations of England and Portugal*, published in 1907. The relevant section of their work is mainly concerned with the political background and with institutional and treaty questions, and on these subjects it is still of much value. But little interest is shown in the overall movements of the trade or in their underlying causes, while it naturally lacks the

[1] C. Nettels, op. cit., *passim*; V. L. Brown, *A.H.R.*, Vol. XXXI (1926), pp. 669, 673-4; G. H. Nelson, op. cit., *passim*; A. Christelow, *H.A.H.R.*, Vol. XXII (1942), *passim*; L. S. Sutherland, *A London Merchant, 1695-1774* (Oxford, 1933), pp. 19-22.

[2] See Chapter 1, p. 33; Chapter 2, p. 47.

[3] R. Pares, op. cit., *passim*, and *Yankees and Creoles* (1956), *passim*.

insights to be gained from later studies by Portuguese historians. The other study of note, Miss L. S. Sutherland's *A London Merchant, 1695-1774* (1933), deals with one man's business with Portugal in the mid-eighteenth century and is inherently restricted in scope. It is hoped that this gap in our knowledge of the English 'Commercial Revolution' will, in part at least, be filled by the study which follows.[1]

In the late seventeenth century, Portugal and Brazil's significance for English trade was very moderate. In the years 1662-3 and 1668-9[2] exports to Portugal from London averaged only £156,000, while imports into London came to £77,000: the outports, however, also dealt to some extent with Portugal. London's trade consisted mainly of the exchange of woollen manufactures, especially serges and bays, for Brazilian sugar and Portuguese oil and fruit.[3] In the 1670s and 1680s English exports probably fell away to even lower levels with the onset of commercial depression in Brazil and Portugal – brought about by the rise of West Indian sugar production – and the import restrictions and attempts to develop home industry which the Portuguese historian, Magalhães Godinho, argues were inspired by the depression.[4] But, as is discussed below, the later 1690s saw Brazilian commerce revive, and for the next sixty years or so Portugal enjoyed remarkable commercial prosperity. This prosperity led to the abandonment of the policy of industrial expansion, and until the

[1] Little discussion will be found in the following pages of the English merchant communities, as such, in England or Portugal, or of the commercial treaties between the two countries or the numerous disputes arising from them. Such discussion has been limited, partly because my approach has been concerned with other themes, and partly because such matters have been treated in some detail in the work by Shillington and Chapman already cited, and in other studies, notably, Sir Richard Lodge, 'The English Factory at Lisbon. Some Chapters in its History', *Transactions of the Royal Historical Society*, 4th series, Vol. XVI (1933) and A. R. Walford, *The British Factory in Lisbon* (Lisbon, 1940).

[2] The two years running from Michaelmas to Michaelmas.

[3] B.M. Add. MSS. 36,785.

[4] V. M. Godinho, 'Flottes du Sucre et Flottes de l'Or (1670-1770)', *Annales*, Vol. V (1950). This article is of great value for understanding the important changes in Portuguese commerce and general economic life between 1670 and 1770. A good discussion of the Portuguese Atlantic economy in the mid seventeenth century is found in F. Mauro, *Le Portugal et l'Atlantique au XVIIe Siècle (1570-1670)* (Paris, 1960), while Portuguese commerce and economic life more generally in the mid-eighteenth century is well treated in J. de Macedo, *A Situação Económica no Tempo de Pombal* (Oporto, 1951). On the general state of Portuguese industry in the late seventeenth and the eighteenth centuries, see also the latter author's *Problemas de História da Indústria Portuguesa no Século XVIII* (Lisbon, 1963).

1760s Portugal's manufacturing interests remained poorly developed. Domestic supplies of mercantile capital were also relatively limited at this time. Nevertheless Portugal pursued orthodox economic policies towards her empire, restricting the growth of manufacturing and reserving trade to her own ports and nationals. Such conditions offered England and the other advanced European nations attractive opportunities for trade, and for much of the period to 1770, as will be seen, the importance of Portugal and Brazil for English trade and for the English economy more generally was not only considerable but increasingly so.

The following study also illuminates the great and growing diversity in the contemporary organization of English foreign trade. With the curtailing of the privileges of the Merchant Adventurers and the Eastland Company in the late seventeenth century, the only important branches still controlled by companies were those with the Levant and Asia. The individual merchant trading on his own account or in partnership had become the predominant unit of enterprise. But beneath this growing uniformity, business practice was diverse. Commercial growth from the mid-seventeenth century had increased the possibilities of specialization open to merchants in terms of both areas and commodities, while the practical problems presented by trade with many different regions and the widening range of commodities resulted in greatly differing business methods. The trade with Portugal illustrates the wide range of practice that could be found in a single branch of commerce.

Light is thrown too on the structure and evolution of the English Atlantic economy. By 1700, with the growth of English colonial commerce, a multilateral system of trade, shipping and payments existed in the Atlantic, centring on the plantation economies of the West Indies and the more southerly of the American mainland colonies, and including the northern mainland colonies and the West African slave stations. As will be seen, English and colonial-American commerce with Portugal added notably to the range and efficiency of this system.

Finally, the study makes some contribution to our understanding of the nature of fluctuations in eighteenth-century trade, both of a seasonal and yearly nature. In his consideration of yearly fluctuations in English trade as a whole in this century, Professor Ashton pointed to war as the chief cause of instability.[1] In the Portugal trade war was undoubtedly an important cause of fluctuations, but emphasis needs to be centred on a broader and more general range of factors bound up with movements in production.

[1] T. S. Ashton, *Economic Fluctuations in England, 1700-1800* (Oxford, 1959), p. 56.

THE COURSE OF ANGLO-PORTUGUESE TRADE 1700-1770

1 *Expansion to 1760*

THIS STUDY IS concerned with the trades conducted between England and Portugal and the English North American colonies and Portugal in the first seventy years of the eighteenth century. English commerce with Madeira has been excluded,[1] but attention is given to the English interests in the Portuguese trades with the Mediterranean and northern Europe.[2]

Over the years from 1700 to 1770, according to the official English trade figures, the commerce between England and Portugal underwent striking change. As can be seen in Figures 1 and 2, and Table II below, a period of vigorous growth to about 1740 was followed by some years of broad stability which ended with a burst of renewed growth in the later 1750s, and then, in the 1760s, by an absolute and pronounced decline.[3] The period of overall expansion of the trade to 1760 will be examined in this chapter, and the marked decline of the 1760s in the following chapter. As will be seen, the factors underlying the growth of the trade and its subsequent decline were both European and American in nature, in part the result of commercial and political rivalries in Europe, but mainly the result of a long-term increase, and subsequent decline, in Portuguese and Brazilian prosperity.

In the export trade from England the first forty years of the century

[1] Direct trade between England and Madeira remained minor in this period, official values of annual English exports only once exceeding £100,000 and being usually well below £50,000 while annual imports never rose above £10,000. C. Whitworth, *State of the Trade of Great Britain*, Part II, pp. 23-4. Madeira's significance for English overseas trade at this time largely lay in its position in the English Atlantic trading system, as a market for Pennsylvanian grain and New England cod and a principal source of the wines drunk in the mainland colonies and the West Indies.

[2] See Chapter 9.

[3] Despite the weaknesses of the official English trade statistics (there are no comparable Portuguese figures) there are grounds for thinking that they offer a reasonable if approximate guide to the actual general movements in the trade. See below, p. 140, 'Note on the use of the official English trade statistics'.

FIGURE 1. Annual movements in the trade between England and Portugal, 1697-1773. After C. Whitworth, *State of the Trade of Great Britain*, part II, pp. 27-8 (London, 1776). For the annual figures see Appendix I.

saw a near doubling of the value of transactions. Then, after a period of comparative stability in the 1740s and early 1750s, renewed growth produced an overall peak in exports of £1,301,000 annually between 1756 and 1760. Throughout the years to 1760 English re-exports of foreign and colonial goods to Portugal remained small, average annual values on the basis of five-year periods between 1700 and 1760 varying from a maximum of £52,000 in 1736-40 to as little as £22,000 in the late 1750s.[1] Amongst such re-exports German and Dutch linens, pipe staves, rice and dried Newfoundland cod were most prominent.

[1] For the value of re-exports for most of the five-year periods between 1700 and 1760, see Appendix II. The figures for the groups of products and individual products in the trade given in the pages below have been drawn from P.R.O. Customs 3. It should be remembered that the official values used here and below to indicate the relative importance of products no more than approximate to the actual values.

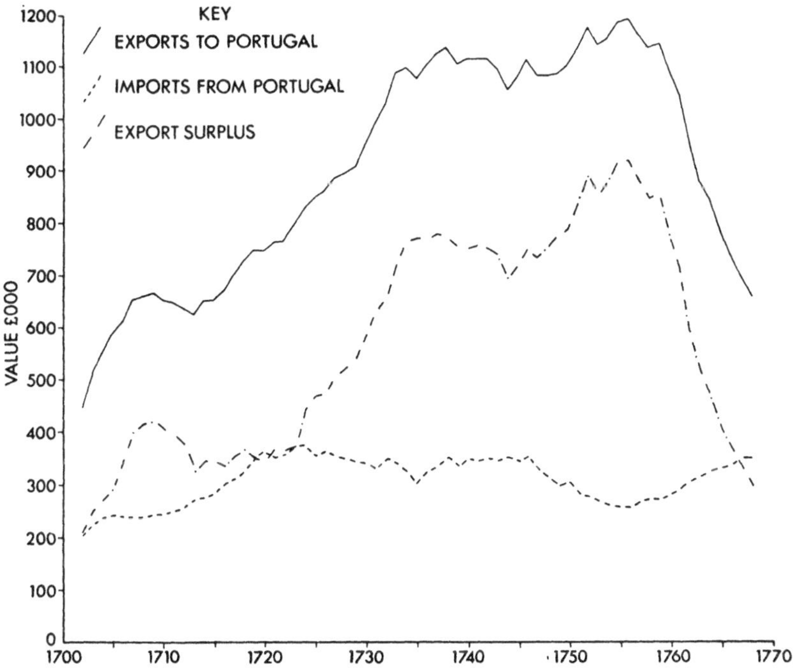

FIGURE 2. Trends in the trade between England and Portugal, 1702-1768. Derived from eleven-year geometric moving averages of the data shown in Figure 1.

Thus the great increase in exports to Portugal depended entirely on shipments of English products.

Of the English products shipped to Portugal, textiles were by far the most important group. When averaged for five-year periods between 1700 and 1760 the value of the principal textiles exported as a proportion of total exports never fell below 70 per cent and at their maximum attained a level of 84 per cent.[1] Woollen and worsted fabrics predominated, especially the lighter and more moderately priced. Bays, a semi-worsted fabric, led among the various items, their export averaging £159,000 annually in 1706-10, £435,000 in 1736-40, and £443,000 in 1756-60. Early in the century shipments of perpetuanas and serges ranked second, averaging £109,000 in 1706-1710, but after 1714, and especially after 1724, their sales declined. By the early 1720s worsted stuff shipments had taken second place,

[1] For the position in each five-year period, and for the textiles included, see Appendix III.

averaging £172,000 annually in 1736-40 and £167,000 in the late 1750s. Until 1740 the finer quality cloths had only a limited sale, exports of short, long and Spanish cloths together in most years being

Table II THE TRADE BETWEEN ENGLAND AND PORTUGAL, 1698-1775 (£ THOUSANDS: ANNUAL AVERAGES)

	Exports to Portugal	*Imports from Portugal*	*Export surplus*
1698-1702	355	200	155
1700-4	514	254	260
1701-5	610	242	368
1706-10	652	240	413
1711-15	638	252	385
1716-20	695	349	346
1721-5	811	387	424
1726-30	914	359	555
1731-5	1,024	326	698
1736-40	1,164	301	864
1741-5	1,115	429	687
1746-50	1,114	324	790
1751-5	1,098	272	826
1756-60	1,301	257	1,044
1761-5	965	314	650
1766-70	595	356	239
1771-5	613	365	248

Source: C. Whitworth, *State of the Trade of Great Britain*, Part II, pp. 27-8. (The annual totals for the trade printed by Whitworth were drawn by him from the Ledgers of the Inspectors-General, P.R.O. Customs 3. His 1713 export figure has been corrected to £628,000.)

well below £100,000; afterwards shipments of the first two underwent some growth, and between 1756 and 1760 averaged respectively £155,000 and £100,000 annually. The sale of worsted stockings also grew markedly over the period from an annual average of £30,000 in 1706-10 to £67,000 in 1736-40, and £80,000 in 1756-60, as did the trade in hats made of felt, beaver and castor, whose annual value in the same periods came to £14,000, £78,000 and £89,000 respectively. Minor consignments of silk goods, linens and cottons were also made, together with a great miscellany of non-textile manufactures, the most important being wrought iron wares which averaged some £20,000 annually by 1756-60. The others included nails and barrel hoops; brass, copper and pewter articles; gunpowder; cordage; copperas; paper; looking-glasses, bottles and other glassware; tanned leather; furniture; and watches and clocks. Lead, lead shot and tin were also exported in minor quantities, together with quite sizeable shipments of coal.[1]

Grainstuffs – wheat, barley, oats and rye – and malt and flour were also shipped in quantity from England to Portugal.[2] Wheat cargoes were invariably the most valuable, at their peak, in 1731-5, averaging some 92,000 quarters annually, valued at £124,000. In these years wheat shipments accounted for 12 per cent by value of all exports to Portugal, and in no other five-year period between 1700 and 1760 than 1716-20, except possibly 1726-30, did their share fall below 5 per cent.[3] Butter, cheese, fish (mostly herrings and pilchards), cider, ale and strong beer were also shipped out in small quantities.

Statistics are much scarcer for the trade from Newfoundland and English North America to Portugal, but they suggest no great increase in activity over the first sixty years of the century. Shipments of dried cod (*bacalhau*) from Newfoundland and to a much smaller extent from Boston and other New England ports were the largest items.[4] In 1707 Charles Davenant estimated the Newfoundland cod imports into Portugal and Spain together at £130,000 annually,[5] and in June 1729 an English merchant in Lisbon estimated the total yearly sale in Portugal at 50,000 quintals worth £55,000.[6] A month or two later these latter figures were declared too low by another

[1] From 1720 coal exports usually came to between 1-2,000 chaldrons annually, their value being of the order of £1,500-3,000 annually.

[2] Throughout the period to 1770 Portugal was a large net importer of grainstuffs. See V. Magalhães Godinho, *Prix et Monnaies au Portugal, 1750-1850* (Paris, 1955), pp. 147-9. In 1765 the English Merchants in Lisbon thought Portugal's production of wheat, barley and flour 'one Year with another . . . scarcely sufficient for the Maintenance of its Inhabitants for six Months; they are therefore obliged to be supplied from abroad with large quantities'. Lisbon Factory memorial, 24 July 1765, P.R.O. C.O. 388/95, I.2.

[3] For their share in most five-year periods, see Appendix IV. Annual wheat exports are depicted in Figure 5, p. 116. As is discussed in Chapter 4, pp. 66-7, grain shipments to Portugal were often made on a somewhat speculative basis, masters of vessels receiving 'open' instructions to find the best markets for their cargoes. Since Lisbon was a major centre for market intelligence in southern Europe, it may be that part of the grain declared for Portugal was in fact carried on to Spain or elsewhere. However, this may have been compensated by grain cargoes which although declared for Spain or elsewhere were in fact unloaded in Portugal.

[4] In 1721 it was said that New Hampshire's 'best and most merchantable fish' was exported to Portugal and Italy. *Cal. S.P. Col. (A.W.I.)* 1720-1, p. 411.

[5] *Journal of Trade*, 1704-1708/9, p. 427.

[6] Taken from a survey of Anglo-Portuguese trade attached to Tyrawly to Newcastle, 26 June 1729, P.R.O. S.P. 89/35. A further copy is in B.N. Col. Pomb., Cod. 638, ff. 461-2. A quintal was approximately one cwt.

English merchant who considered imports never fell below 80,000 quintals worth £88,000.[1] New York, Pennsylvania and Maryland conducted an intermittent trade in wheat, maize and flour with Portugal but this remained small at this time, their surplus grain usually being shipped to the West Indies.[2] In 1729 the 'Corn, Flower or Bread from Maryland, New York &c.' sent to Portugal was estimated at only £8,250 annually.[3] Timber and pipe staves from New Hampshire and the other northern colonies,[4] and, for a time, rice from South Carolina,[5] were also shipped to Portugal in small quantities. As well as goods, the colonial vessels carrying them were sometimes sold to the Portuguese.[6] While these other trades (excluding the cod trade) were not significant quantitatively before the 1760s, the shipping they employed nevertheless played a notable part in the overall organization of Anglo-Portuguese trade.[7]

On the other hand, official imports into England from Portugal (that is, excluding bullion which entered unrecorded by the Customs) followed a quite different course between 1700 and 1760. The figures in Table II indicate some limited growth around 1700, followed by further growth after 1715 which brought import values to some £387,000 annually in 1721-5; thereafter imports remained broadly stable at a level somewhat below this figure until the 1750s when they fell back to below £300,000 annually. Sugar imports, formerly so important, had ceased, and wines now dominated the cargoes from Portugal, their share of total imports by value in the five-year periods between 1700 and 1760 varying between 69 per cent in 1700-4 and

[1] Paper attached to Compton to Newcastle, 6 August 1729 N.S., P.R.O. S.P. 89/35. A further survey made in London, probably in 1730, put fish imports annually at 80,000 quintals worth £66,000. B.N. Col. Pomb., Cod. 638, f. 455. Both this survey and that cited in the previous footnote are printed in part in J. Lucio de Azevedo, *Épocas de Portugal Economico* (Lisbon, 1947), 2nd edition, pp. 486-7.

[2] On these trades, see *Cal. S.P. Col.* (*A.W.I.*), 1708-9, p. 477; 1712-14, p. 368; 1716-17, p. 271; 1720-1, pp. 130, 210; and 1731, p. 231.

[3] Paper attached to Compton to Newcastle, 6 August 1729 N.S., P.R.O. S.P. 89/35.

[4] In 1700 a former Governor of New Hampshire observed that some of its inhabitants had contracted to send timber to Portugal 'for building great ships and are . . . felling the best masts in the Province'. *Cal. S.P. Col.* (*A.W.I.*), 1700, p. 32. And in 1701 it was said a 'great deal' of timber was annually transported from Piscataqua in Massachusetts to Portugal. Ibid., 1701, p. 576. See also ibid., 1720-1, p. 210, and 1731, pp. 231, 360.

[5] From 1705 until 1735 rice was an enumerated commodity.

[6] See *Cal. S.P. Col.* (*A.W.I.*), 1720-1, p. 210, which refers to this being practised by the Philadelphia merchants.

[7] See Chapter 6.

88 per cent in 1731-5, and being generally over 80 per cent.[1] The remaining imports were virtually all primary products of Portuguese origin. They included various fruits – oranges, lemons, figs and olives – olive oil, salt, cork and shumack. Brazilwood and one or two more exotic items such as 'elephants teeth' (ivory) and leopard skins emanating from Brazil and the Portuguese colonies in Africa were also imported. None of these lesser products had a substantial trade in terms of their value, imports of oranges and lemons for example averaging only £9,000 annually in the late 1750s, although in volume terms their trade was not negligible.[2] Exports from Portugal direct to the English North American colonies generally remained small, consisting largely of salt for the Newfoundland and New England fisheries, some illegal wine shipments, and, occasionally, Portuguese coin,[3] the American balances in the main being remitted to merchants' agents in England.[4]

According to the official English figures England achieved a surplus in her visible trade with Portugal in every year between 1700 and 1760.[5] Over the period it grew decidedly: in no five-year period before 1720, as shown in Table II, did it fall below £250,000 annually, after 1721-5 it never fell below £500,000, and in the late 1750s it averaged over a million pounds annually. For the reasons already indicated,[6] these official surpluses were probably larger than the real surpluses, and whenever the former were small, there was almost certainly a visible trade deficit. But considerable sums also accrued to England each year from her 'invisible' trades with Portugal, principally the employment of a large and growing capital by English merchants in the credit granted to textile purchasers in Portugal,[7] the sale of Newfoundland cod by West of England fishermen, the use of English

[1] For their share in each five-year period, and tunnage and value figures, see Appendix V.

[2] In 1756-60 imports of oranges and lemons averaged some 14,300 thous. annually, and imports of cork and shumack, 9,300 and 6,800 cwts. annually respectively.

[3] See, for example, *Cal. H. of L. MSS.*, 1699-1702 (Vol. IV), p. 448, *Cal. S.P. Col.* (*A.W.I.*), 1702-3, pp. 204, 220; 1706-8, p. 608; 1720-1, p. 130; 1735-6, pp. 69-70.

[4] See below, Chapter 4.

[5] For the annual figures, see Appendix I.

[6] See below, 'Note on the use of the official English statistics', p. 140. To the extent that grain declared for Portugal was unloaded elsewhere, official export values and hence the official surpluses were overstated. The sums involved, however, would have been small.

[7] See below, Chapters 3 and 9. As is discussed in Chapter 3 English merchants dominated the supply of textiles to Portugal.

ships in Portugal's colonial and foreign commerce,[1] and the English merchants' varied interests as principals in other branches of Portuguese trade and economic life.[2] These earnings would have gone far towards offsetting the exaggeration of the official surplus down to 1750,[3] so that on current trade account as a whole England may well have enjoyed surpluses not very much different from the official figures.

These recurrent surpluses could have been settled in three main ways – through English investment, by payments made through a third country, or in bullion. Some English investment in vineyards and shipping did occur but only in a fairly small way:[4] more important was the likely employment of part of the English trade balances each year in expanding the commercial credit granted to the Portuguese and in financing English interests in other branches of Portuguese commerce. There is no evidence of substantial payments made via Holland or any other third country.[5] In consequence the English surpluses were, in the main, regularly settled in bullion, an arrangement as much deplored by the Portuguese as it was extolled by Englishmen. After allowing for the items which dispensed with or negotiated the actual settlement of the English surpluses, the bullion shipped to England in this way may have reached £25,000,000 between 1700 and 1760, an estimate, however, necessarily very approximate.[6] The exchange rate of a nation habitually exporting gold should normally be at gold export point, and this is borne out in Portugal's case in these years by reference to the London rate on Lisbon[7] (unfortunately the Lisbon rates on London are not available). If gold export point is

[1] See below, Chapter 9.

[2] See below, Chapter 9.

[3] Imports from Portugal were very largely carried in English vessels and insured in London which reduces the significance of the official exclusion of freight and insurance payments on imports.

[4] See below, Chapter 9.

[5] Portugal apparently had visible trade deficits with all the chief European nations. *Mercator's Letters on Portugal and its Commerce* (1754), pp. 11-15. See also the survey of Portugal's trade referred to above, p. 17n., and Burnett to Craggs, 10 April 1720 N.S., P.R.O. S.P. 89/28.

[6] Allowance is made here too for the English subsidies paid to Portugal, and English military expenditures there, during the War of the Spanish Succession. On these subsidies and payments, see further below, p. 38. Allowance is also made for the unrecorded traffic in diamonds to England from Portugal which began towards the end of the 1720s. See below, p. 24.

[7] J. Castaing, *Course of the Exchange*. The exchange was given as shillings and pence for the *milreis*.

taken as 5s. 5¾d.,[1] then in all but twenty years between 1700 and 1760 the annual London rate of exchange (average of the first rate quoted each month) stood at this level or below, and in only eight years, 1700-6 and 1717, did no first-monthly rate fail to do so.[2] In 1700 and 1701 England's trade may have been in deficit, but in 1702-6 the official surplus ranged from £266,000 to £596,000. This discrepancy probably sprang from the abnormal conditions in the bullion and exchange markets during the War of the Spanish Succession, in particular from the subsidies paid to Portugal and the English military expenditures there.[3] Special circumstances must also have applied in 1717. If, on the other hand, the gold export point is taken as 5s. 6·01d. for this period, then in only fourteen years was the annual rate of exchange above it, and in only seven, 1700-6, did no first-monthly quotation ever fall as low. To some extent the Portuguese *milreis* was depressed by the practice by which Portuguese trading debts with other countries were settled by bills of exchange drawn on London, but this would have had only a marginal influence.[4]

English commercial remittances did not constitute the entire bullion trade to England from Portugal. Shipments based on Dutch, German and other European nations' trading surpluses with Portugal were also made to England throughout the period. This was because of the far greater availability of English vessels at Lisbon sailing northwards, especially armed vessels with diplomatic immunity from search, compared with other countries, and also because of the special bullion dealing services offered by English houses in Lisbon. In

[1] In 1721 *The British Merchant*, quoted without correction in the early 1750s by M. Postlethwayt, *The Universal Dictionary of Trade and Commerce* (1751-5), put the gold export point at under 5s. 6d. See L. S. Sutherland, op. cit., p. 30. Other sources, probably later, put it at 5s. 6·01d., par being 5s. 7½d., ibid. On the basis of Sir Isaac Newton's valuations the par of exchange was 5s. 7·166d., M. Decker, *An Essay on the Causes of the Decline of the Foreign Trade* (1744), p. 88, and [N. Magens], *The Universal Merchant* (1753), p. 82. In 1766 par was put at 5s. 7½d., *Money of England reduced into Money of Portugal* (Falmouth, 1766). The little information available on the Lisbon rates of exchange indicate that they were generally above the London rate by up to a 1d. the *milreis*. See L. S. Sutherland, op. cit., p. 30.

[2] The first January quotation on Lisbon each year, and the annual average of the first rate quoted each month are given in Appendix VI.

[3] In August 1705 it was noted in Lisbon that 'the Exchange [is] very much risen by the severall credits which are sent hither for the Navy Victuall & Transport Offices & the Dutch taking up all the money in order to pay the arrears of the subsidys'. Letter to C. Hedges, 12 August 1705 N.S., P.R.O. S.P. 89/18, f. 303. On these payments, see below, p. 38.

[4] See below, Chapter 7.

1729 an English merchant in Lisbon declared that part of the bullion outflow settling Portugal's trading debts with other European countries went directly to Italy and 'the Rest for the most part by the way of England on account of the Conveniences of the Exchange and of Shipping'.[1] This may exaggerate England's importance as an entrepôt, but it seems clear that a very considerable part of European bullion balances in Portugal was remitted homewards in this way.[2] One contemporary, in fact, thought the foreign bullion transfers composed the 'greatest part' of all the bullion exported to England,[3] while the great relative value of that shipped on the basis of Dutch trade was stressed by Sir Mathew Decker,[4] and another writer observed that 'a great Part of the Gold and Silver remitted to England from Spain and Portugal is the Return of Goods from Germany'.[5] The first writer, however, was especially concerned with minimizing English responsibility for the drain of bullion from Portugal and it is likely that all their remarks need to be interpreted with caution. Although precise measurement is out of the question it is probable that in most years English commercial remittances composed substantially the larger element because of England's much greater trade with Portugal compared with other countries.[6] A few figures survive of the bullion brought by the packet-boats to Falmouth from Lisbon: between 25 March 1740 and 8 June 1741 its value came to £447,347,[7]

[1] Attachment to Tyrawly to Newcastle, 26 June 1729, P.R.O. S.P. 89/35; B.N. Col. Pomb., Cod. 638, f. 461.

[2] See *Mercator's Letters on Portugal and its Commerce*, pp. 37-8, and *Description de la Ville de Lisbonne* (Paris, 1730), pp. 267-8. For figures of the English and foreign shipping clearing Lisbon between 1746 and 1770 see J. de Macedo, 'Portugal e a Económia Pombalina: Temas e Hipóteses', *Rev. de H.*, Vol. IX (1954), p. 99. The armed and diplomatically privileged English ships were the Falmouth-Lisbon packet-boats and men-of-war. This matter is further treated in Chapter 7.

[3] *Mercator's Letters on Portugal and its Commerce*, p. 38.

[4] Op. cit., p. 89. See also A. Anderson, *An Historical and Chronological Deduction of the Origin of Commerce* (1764), Vol. I, Introduction, p. x.

[5] [N. Magens], *The Universal Merchant*, p. 67.

[6] See below, pp. 34-5. If, as is likely, Ireland in its trade with Portugal also enjoyed a favourable balance, then no doubt some of the bullion shipped from Portugal in its settlement went directly to England. Payments for Irish shipments to Portugal were also made by bill on London, see M. Decker, op. cit., p. 89, which would have further helped to depress the *milreis*. The sums involved in both cases, however, would have been small, in 1729 Ireland's exports to Portugal, principally camblets and butter, being estimated at only some £52,000 annually. Paper attached to Compton to Newcastle, 6 August 1729 N.S., P.R.O. S.P. 89/35.

[7] Chol. (H.) MSS. Cambridge. P. 44, 50, and P. 89, 17/1. (Internal evidence indicates that all the packet-boats listed in P. 89, 17/1, arrived in 1741.)

while in the calendar years 1759 and 1760 it totalled £787,290 and £1,085,559 respectively.[1] This certainly understates the total bullion inflow into England in these years, however, since in wartime warships were much resorted to for safer carriage, while merchant ships were also employed.[2]

Throughout the period to 1760 the bullion transferred from Portugal consisted principally of gold, chiefly in the form of Portuguese coin but also in bar and dust. Gold, for example, composed the larger part by far (in value) of the bullion brought by the Falmouth packets between January and June 1741.[3] After 1747 when the Portuguese mint ratio of gold to silver was 13·6 to 1 compared to the English ratio of 15·21 to 1, this is as would be expected: but before 1747 the Portuguese ratio was 16·25 to 1 compared to England's 15·57 to 1 until 1717 and 15·21 to 1 thereafter,[4] which indicates silver as the precious metal to be exported. The predominance of gold shipments nevertheless is mainly explained by the greater profit in shipping silver from Portugal to Asia, which made silver scarce in Portugal and sufficiently raised its market value in relation to gold to lead to the latter's use in European transfers.[5] Until 1714 the import of gold would also have been fostered by the official English valuation

[1] B.N. Col. Pomb., Cod. 635, f. 445. (The 1760 total in this document is slightly wrong through faulty addition and has been corrected.)

[2] See below, Chapter 7.

[3] Chol. (H). MSS. P. 89, 17/1. See also B.M. Add. MSS. 23,634, ff. 49, 74, and L. S. Sutherland, op. cit., p. 36.

[4] T. S. Ashton, *An Economic History of England: The 18th Century* (1955), p. 171; W. A. Shaw, *The History of Currency* (n. d.), p. 273.

[5] In 1730 John Conduitt observed 'by reason of [the] high valuation of gold, and low valuation of silver, there has been no silver coined or current [in Portugal] for several years last past, though but twenty years ago it was in greater plenty than gold. To supply the want of it, they coin pieces of gold of several denominations . . . and a great quantity of copper money. . . . Though a mark of silver at Lisbon produces at the mint only 6,400 *rees*, yet without considering the high price it bears when the Portuguese East-India ships are going out, it is not to be bought at a medium, one time with another, under 7,200 *rees* which reduces the real proportion between silver and gold in Portugal as 14 lb 2 oz 13 dwt 8 grs of fine silver is to one pound weight of fine gold.' *Observations upon the Present State of our Gold and Silver Coins* (1730), reprinted in W. A. Shaw, *Select Tracts and Documents illustrative of English Monetary History, 1626-1730* (1935), p. 188. In 1720 the English Consul in Lisbon had remarked on the possibility of the Portuguese Crown coining in silver 'about two Millions of Crowns (. . . of near three Shillings English) for the Current Use of their Marketts. This will be . . . of Service . . . to our Trade, for now it is almost impossible to get change for a [gold] Moeda.' Burnett to Craggs, 21 April 1720 N.S., P.R.O. S.P. 89/28.

of the Portuguese gold *moeda* at 28s. each, overvaluing them by 5d.[1]

As well as these bullion shipments, note also needs to be taken of another traffic from Portugal to England which was unrecorded by the English Customs – that in diamonds. This came into being towards the end of the 1720s. In 1730 reference was made to the 'great Quantity of Diamonds taken by the English' from Lisbon,[2] and in 1732, according to the English Envoy in Lisbon, 'much the greater part of the Diamonds that come from the Brasils have hitherto gone to London', on account of the greater availability of English shipping compared to other countries, the diamonds being distributed from London 'to the rest of Europe'.[3] This traffic from Portugal is likely to have fluctuated considerably, because of variations in supply in Portugal and because of the competition of Amsterdam in this business, and in some years to have been at a low level only. The only figures of the values involved relate to the 1750s, when the exportation of diamonds from Portugal was in the hands of officially appointed contractors. In the years 1753-5 and 1757-60 when London merchant houses held the contracts, the business averaged respectively about £107,000 and £72,000 annually.[4]

The factors underlying the general expansion of Anglo-Portuguese trade in the years to 1760 fall into two main groups: those behind the rise and subsequent maintenance of a large Portuguese wine trade to England, and those accounting for the expansion of English textile shipments to Portugal and the return flow of bullion.

Portuguese wines have been imported into England since at least the fourteenth century, but the rise and subsequent maintenance of a large trade really date from the last decade of the seventeenth century, with the intensification of Anglo-French commercial and political rivalry. The growing discrimination against French wines obliged Englishmen to a very considerable degree, and probably

[1] See Sir Isaac Newton, *State of the Gold and Silver Coin*, 25 September 1717, reprinted in W. A. Shaw, *Select Tracts and Documents illustrative of English Monetary History*, pp. 170-1. See also Sir John Craig, *The Mint* (Cambridge, 1953), p. 215.

[2] B.N. Col. Pomb., Cod. 638, f. 455.

[3] Tyrawly to Newcastle, 2 May 1732, P.R.O. S.P. 89/37.

[4] J. Lucio de Azevedo, *O Marques de Pombal e a sua Época*, 2nd edition (Lisbon, 1922), p. 113. In the first period Bristow, Ward and Co. held the contract, and in the second, John Gore and Joshua Van Neck. In the 1760s the Dutch merchant Daniel Gil de Meester had the contract.

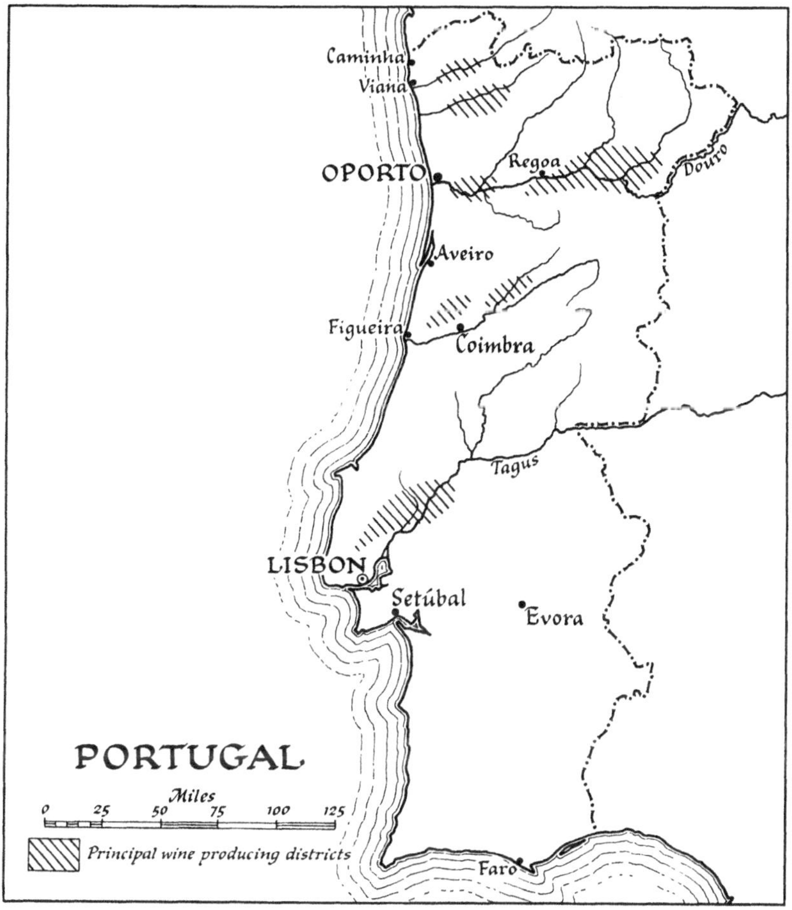
Caminha
Viana
OPORTO
Regoa
Douro
Aveiro
Figueira
Coimbra
Tagus
LISBON
Setúbal
Evora
Faro
PORTUGAL
Miles
0 25 50 75 100 125
Principal wine producing districts

reluctantly, to forgo claret and other French wines for the wines of Portugal. The Customs figures suggest that a substantial Portuguese trade began between 1678 and 1685, when French trade was placed under a general embargo.[1] During these years imports of French wines, previously the chief wines imported, apparently ceased, being replaced by shipments from elsewhere, particularly Spain and Portugal. Between 1675 and 1678 imports of Portuguese wines into London averaged only 120 tuns annually, but between 1679 and 1685 they rose sharply to 6,880 tuns annually.[2] Almost certainly though these imports were mostly French wines falsely entered. Contemporary opinion suggests that the direction of the Court and the connivance of Customs officials led to much fraudulent entry,[3] and this is supported by figures of Oporto's wine exports at this time which remained low although the city served one of the most important Portuguese wine producing regions.[4] And with the lifting of the prohibition in 1685 French wines immediately regained a leading position while Portuguese imports returned to a low level.

On the outbreak of war with France in 1689, however, French wine imports were again prohibited,[5] and from this year dates the substantial trade in Portuguese wines. This time the official expansion of Portuguese imports into England was matched by much increased shipments from Oporto: between 1690 and 1696 imports into London averaged 5,490 tuns annually while Oporto's exports rose to an average 4,660 tuns. This view is supported by a contemporary observation of about 1701 that 'these port-wines [came] into Esteem in England since ye beginn^{g} of ye late war',[6] and, some years later, by *The British Merchant* which observed that the war which began in 1689 'holding so exceeding long, the Portugal merchants soon enlarged their Trade, and filled the whole Nation with their Wines'. The changeover was not without some strain, for, the account

[1] Imposed by 29 and 30 Charles II c.1, ended by 1 James II c.6.

[2] See V. M. Shillington and A. B. W. Chapman, op. cit., Appendix II (IV).

[3] See E. Lipson, *The Economic History of England* (6th edition, 1956), Vol. III, p. 105.

[4] Oporto's wine exports from 1678 are printed in J. Warre, *The Past, Present and probably the Future State of the Wine Trade* (1823), Appendix M. The English figures of Portuguese wines entering London between 1678 and 1685 also indicate something odd: from 1-2,000 tuns annually in 1678-81 they rose sharply to 13,860 tuns in 1682 and 16,770 in 1683, fell back to only 1,610 the next year and rose again to 12,190 in 1685.

[5] 1 William & Mary c.34, renewed in 1692 for a further three years by 4 William & Mary c.25.

[6] B.M. Add. MSS. 23,726, f. 18.

continues, the Portuguese wines being 'heavy and strong, did not at first please, and we hanker'd after the old claret of Bourdeaux; but in time . . . the Merchants found Ways and Means either to bring the Portuguese Wine to our Palates, or Custom brought our Palates to the Wine: So that we began to forget the French Wines, and like the others well enough'.[1] Of the imports from elsewhere those from Spain also grew considerably, shipments into London rising to 6,250 tuns annually between 1690 and 1696.

During the peace of 1697-1702 French wines could again freely enter England. Nevertheless their official trade failed to revive and both Portuguese and Spanish imports continued at a high level.[2] This sprang directly from the policy under William III of sharply increasing import duties on French products. In 1685 a tun of wine from France, Portugal or Spain paid about the same duty; when imported into London by a British merchant in a British vessel this was respectively £18. 6s., £18. 11s. and £19. 7s.[3] By the peace of 1697, however, the duty on French wines had been raised to £53. 1s. a tun, while Portuguese and Spanish wines paid only £22. 12s. and £23. 8s. respectively. Thus, some six years before the Methuen treaty was signed in 1703, Portuguese wines already had a tariff preference of over 50 per cent.[4] This preference for Iberian wines was maintained in 1703 and 1704 when further tariff increases were made,[5] and with the failure of Bolingbroke's attempt to remove it in 1712-13 it persisted till the Eden treaty of 1786.[6] In this decided tariff preference for Iberian wine lies the essential explanation of the continuing low level of French wine imports during the eighteenth century.

[1] C. King (ed.), *The British Merchant* (1721), Vol. II, p. 277. On the evolution in the nature of port wine in the eighteenth century, see Chapter 5.

[2] The contraband trade in French wines cannot be measured, but although without question notable, is unlikely to have been great because of the product's bulkiness.

[3] The tun filled for sale and duties payable immediately.

[4] As Miss M. E. Turner has pointed out modern research has tended to whittle down the importance formerly given to the Methuen treaty by historians. In an interesting revaluation of its significance she considers its only importance for the Portuguese wine trade lay perhaps in the guarantee it gave of a continual tariff preference. See Chapter II of her unpublished University of Oxford D.Phil. thesis, 'Anglo-Portuguese Relations and the War of the Spanish Succession' (1952).

[5] By 1704 the duties on French, Portuguese and Spanish wines were respectively £57. 6s., £26. 13s., and £27. 9s. a tun.

[6] The duty on French wines was raised by £8 a tun in 1745 and by a further £8 in 1763, while Portuguese and Spanish wines became liable to an additional £4 on each occasion.

From the 1690s to 1760 Portugal and Spain provided the great bulk of the wines drunk in England. But whereas in the 1690s the trade from Spain usually surpassed that from Portugal, thereafter Portuguese imports were normally greater by a comfortable and increasing margin.[1] Import duties clearly had no part in this change since they were broadly similar throughout. Two factors, however, may be pointed to. First, Portuguese wine producers may have been better placed than their Spanish competitors to expand the production of red wines capable of serving as tolerable substitutes for claret. And secondly, during the two major Anglo-Spanish wars of the period the supply of Spanish wines was much restricted. This was especially significant in the War of the Spanish Succession. Between 1703 and 1708 official Spanish wine imports into England fell to an average 2,900 tuns annually and did not recover till 1710: their restricted availability at a time when wine-drinking habits were being transformed by the limited supply and high cost of French wines undoubtedly promoted the taste for Portuguese wines. During the war of 1739-48, and especially from 1741, Spanish trade was even more seriously affected,[2] and Portuguese wines, according to the official figures at least, dominated wine imports. In the eight years preceding 1741 Portuguese imports averaged 11,730 tuns annually, some 55 per cent of the total trade; between 1741 and 1748 they rose to 13,550 tuns, just over 90 per cent of the total. Even after bearing in mind the likelihood of Spanish wines falsely entered as Portuguese, and the illegal traffic in French wines, the Portuguese wine trade must have been outstanding in these years. The factors underlying the rise and maintenance of the Portuguese wine trade to England were thus closely associated with England's rivalries with France and, to a lesser extent, Spain. To them must be largely attributed the drinking of port (and the apparent proneness to gout) characteristic of the upper and middle ranks of English society in the eighteenth century.

On the other hand European politics had only a minor bearing on the expansion of textile exports to Portugal between 1700 and 1760 and the growth of bullion imports into England. The explanation of their growth is mainly to be found in the impressive secular expansion

[1] For figures of all wines imported into Great Britain in the eighteenth century, see J. Warre, op. cit., Appendix N.

[2] Between 1741 and 1748 official imports of Spanish wines into England averaged 920 tuns annually compared to 8,620 tuns between 1733 and 1740.

of the Portuguese market for foreign manufactures at this time, and in the greater ability of the English compared to the other northern European manufacturing nations to exploit this situation.

The secular expansion of the Portuguese market for foreign manufactures was closely related to the ending of the depression which had characterized Portuguese commerce in the 1670s and 1680s and the return to a high level of prosperity which, as Magalhães Godinho has shown, began in the 1690s and continued to about 1760.[1] In Portugal itself the development from about 1690 of wine exporting industries in the Douro and Tagus regions and elsewhere, largely in response to increasing English demands,[2] gave a strong impulse to the demand for foreign manufactures. Expanding wine exports meant that employment and incomes were stimulated in the regions concerned and a larger market for manufactures, especially textiles, created and sustained. Moreover, with the revival of commercial prosperity in the 1690s the policy of home industrial expansion which the trade depression of the 1670s and 1680s had inspired was abandoned,[3] and for the next sixty years Portuguese manufacturing interests, with a few exceptions, remained little developed.[4] Increased resort was thus made to foreign supplies of manufactured goods financed at least in part by the foreign balances earned from the expanding wine trade. The process was well observed by an Englishman writing in 1699: 'Its plain y^{t} during the [recent] War ye Planters & Vineyard dressers in Portugal finding greater request of their Wine, sedulously multiplied ye Planting of Vines, & employ'd far greater numbers of people in it than formerly: by wch means there hath been a far greater Exportation of our English Manufactures.'[5] This stimulus to Portuguese purchasing power was reinforced by the population increase taking place: it has been estimated that between 1732 and 1770 the metropolitan population rose from about 2,143,000 to 2,534,000.[6]

1 V. M. Godinho, *Annales* (1950), pp. 188-94.

2 Ibid. pp. 188-9, and J. de Macedo, *A Situação Económica no Tempo de Pombal*, pp. 73-8.

3 V. M. Godinho, *Annales* (1950), pp. 188-9.

4 J. de Macedo, *A Situação Económica no Tempo de Pombal*, pp. 207-210, and *Problemas de História da Indústria Portuguesa no Século XVIII*, *passim*. See also A. Anderson, op. cit., Vol. II, p. 94, and J. Cary, *An Essay towards Regulating the Trades of this Kingdom* (1719), p. 69.

5 P.R.O. S.P. 100/37, f. 47. See also Lisbon Factory memorial, 31 July 1715, P.R.O. C.O. 388/20, P. 71.

6 J. de Macedo, *A Situação Económica no Tempo de Pombal*, p. 200.

More important, however, was the expansion of Portuguese demands for foreign manufactures arising from developments in Brazil. First, there was the remarkable growth of such demands in Brazil itself due to its rapid internal development and in particular the phenomenal rise of gold mining.[1] Until 1690 settlement there was largely confined to the coastal regions of the northern captaincies, with agriculture, especially the plantation cultivation of sugar and to a lesser extent tobacco, the predominant economic activity. The total population at this time has been estimated at between 184,000 and 300,000.[2] In the 1690s gold was discovered in the interior, in what became known as the captaincy of Minas Gerais, and subsequently discoveries were made in other regions. Total output grew quickly: estimates put it at an annual average of 1,500 kg between 1691 and 1700; between 1701 and 1720 it had risen to 2,750 kg annually; in the following twenty years to 8,850 kg and between 1741 and 1760 attained an overall peak of 14,600 kg annually.[3] Diamonds were also found in quantity in Minas Gerais from 1723 onwards.[4] The discovery and working of the gold deposits, and to a notable if far less significant extent, the diamond fields, gave a great impetus to Brazilian economic growth. Boom conditions and an acute labour scarcity led to heavy immigration from Portugal and the large-scale transportation of negro slaves from Africa. Many new settlements were established in the interior, a strong impulse was given to internal trade and it was not long before Rio de Janeiro rivalled Bahia in opulence and importance. By the mid-1760s the colony's population had grown impressively, perhaps to about one and a half millions.[5]

[1] Brazilian economic life at this time is usefully examined in R. C. Simonsen, *Historia Economica do Brasil, 1500-1820* (2 vols., São Paulo, 1937); for a good general account of life in Brazil see C. R. Boxer, *The Golden Age of Brazil, 1695-1750* (Berkeley and Los Angeles, 1962).

[2] Estimate published by Contreira Rodrigues and quoted by R. C. Simonsen, op. cit., Vol. II, p. 51n.

[3] A. Soetbeer, *Edelmetall-Produktion und Werthverhältnis zwischen Gold und Silber* (Gotha, 1879), p. 92, quoted by J. F. Normano, *Brazil. A Study of Economic Types* (Chapel Hill, 1935), p. 31.

[4] The value of the diamonds mined by the official monopolists from 1740 onwards (which necessarily exclude the supply dug illicitly) averaged about £100,000 annually between 1740 and 1752 and about £160,000 annually between 1753 and 1758. C. R. Boxer, op. cit., p. 220.

[5] Estimate published by Thomas Ewbank, *Life in Brazil* (New York, 1856), and quoted by R. C. Simonsen, op. cit., Vol. II, p. 51n. Recent work based on contemporary sources puts the population about 1776 at some 1,800,000. D. Alden, 'The Population

These changed circumstances explain the revival in the value of Brazil's exports to Portugal, which had been in decline since about 1670 following the rise of West Indian sugar production. Statistics of the trade are poor and sparse but Professor Simonsen has indicated that the colony's total exports to Portugal rose from about £2,400,000 in 1700 and £2,500,000 in 1710, to about £4,800,000 in 1760.[1] This was chiefly due to increased gold shipments whose approximate annual value at these three dates was £350,000, £600,000 and £2,200,000 respectively. Thus by 1760 gold exports were almost equal in value to Brazil's other major item of trade, sugar. Additional evidence for greatly expanding gold shipments is provided by the fairly detailed figures compiled by Magalhães Godinho of the gold (excluding contraband) brought to Lisbon from Brazil during the period.[2] These indicate shipments began to grow about 1695 and rose from 725 kg in 1699, to 1,785 kg in 1701, and 4,350 kg in 1703. This upward movement continued in succeeding years, despite some sharp fluctuations. Between 1726 and 1731 the annual shipments were never less than 6-8,000 kg, in the remaining years of the 1730s, except 1732 and 1736, never below 11,000 kg, while in most years between 1740 and 1755 they totalled at least 14,000 kg and sometimes 16,000 kg. Further indications of the great and generally rising value of Brazil's exports to Portugal in the first sixty years of the century can be found in the brief and impressionistic reports of the cargoes of the Brazilian trading fleets made by the English Envoys and Consuls in Lisbon. The cargoes of the Rio de Janeiro fleet, which served the gold mining districts, were stated in 1721 to be 'seldom of less Value than eight hundred thousand pounds';[3] in 1723 the fleet was valued at £1,500,000 of which two-thirds was made up of the registered gold shipments;[4] in 1725 it was said the 'Specie on board the King's ships (besides unregistered Gold and a quantity of Silver which is not declared) amounts to . . . near two Millions Sterling';[5] in 1749 the Rio fleet which arrived in mid-year was 'by all accounts the richest . . .

of Brazil in the Late Eighteenth Century: A Preliminary Survey', *H.A.H.R.*, Vol. XLIII (1963).

[1] Op. cit., Vol. II, graph opposite p. 222.

[2] V. M. Godinho, *Annales* (1950), pp. 192-3.

[3] Burnett to Carteret, 29 November 1721 N.S., P.R.O. S.P. 89/29.

[4] Burnett to Carteret, 18 March 1723 N.S., P.R.O. S.P. 89/30.

[5] Burnett to Newcastle, 19 February 1725 N.S., P.R.O. S.P. 89/31.

for many years. . . . The amount of her Cargo in Treasure and rich Goods is computed to be worth about Two Millions Sterling';[1] and the fleet which arrived at Lisbon in 1753 was 'the richest which ever came from the Brazils, perhaps upon a moderate computation in Gold, Silver and goods to the amount of three Millions Sterling'.[2]

The growth of population and output greatly enlarged effective demand in Brazil for manufactured goods, especially textiles. Since local manufacturing was little developed and subject to restriction, and since Portugal was unable to meet all her colonists' demands herself, considerable recourse was necessarily had to foreign supplies. The Portuguese officially required all European trade with Brazil to be carried on from Portuguese ports alone, and to a very considerable extent this was observed. One major reason for the intermittent and small-scale nature of direct trading by foreigners to Brazil was the lack of any nearby foreign possessions, which would have greatly facilitated its organization. The resultant increased flow of foreign manufactures to Brazil from Lisbon was financed from the sale of Brazilian sugar, tobacco and other agricultural products to European countries, with the balance settled in gold.

The market for foreign manufactures in Portugal also benefited from the impact the growth of Brazilian wealth made on metropolitan Portugal. Lisbon became one of the wealthiest cities in Europe, the Crown and Court were enriched, and profits and employment were provided for a large mercantile class. Other centres with interests in the Brazil trades, particularly Oporto, also gained. The expenditures of the Crown, merchants and others transmitted the commercial prosperity of the period more widely through the Portuguese economy, provided some stimulus to economic activity in general and raised the level of demand in the country for manufactures as well as other commodities.

[1] Castres to Bedford, 12 July 1749 N.S., P.R.O. S.P. 89/47.

[2] Letter of G. Crowle, 12 January 1753, P.R.O. S.P. 89/49. Although the Portuguese trading system called for annual fleets to the main trading regions of Brazil, sometimes, however, fleets for particular regions sailed only once every two or even three years. See Chapter 3, p. 58. Between January 1747 and January 1753 according to the printed lists the registered 'treasure' annually brought to Lisbon from all parts of Brazil was worth on average 12,087,401 *crusados* (*c.* £1,726,770). N.M. [agens], *Further Explanation of some Particular Subjects contained in the Universal Merchant* (1756), pp. 15-16. One contemporary declared that the official registers in Lisbon showed that between 1696 and 1756 bullion to the value of £105,000,000 had been brought to Portugal. *Letters from Portugal on the Late and Present State of that Kingdom* (1777), p. 19.

The development of the notorious contraband trade conducted between southern Brazil and Buenos Aires, a gateway to the extensive Spanish markets in Chile and Peru, was also a contributory factor. This trade became especially active after 1713 when Spain ceded Nova Colonia do Sacramento on the northern shore of the River Plate to Portugal.[1] It consisted mainly in the exchange of manufactures for silver and although its actual size at any time is unknown contemporary opinions suggest it was considerable. In 1736 the Portuguese authorities informed the English Envoy in Lisbon that the trade in English woollen goods alone to Nova Colonia do Sacramento more than equalled the quantities taken by the rest of Brazil,[2] but this was undoubtedly an exaggeration. The trade was particularly buoyant in the mid-1740s when Spain's wartime commerce with America was much interrupted by English naval operations,[3] and was thought to exceed £200,000 annually about 1760 on the basis of the 'annual remittances that came from the Brazils of Spanish silver'.[4] In 1761 the Rio de Janeiro fleet besides bringing to Lisbon ten million *crusados* in gold (*c.* £1,375,000) brought also 'about Four Millions of Crusades in Silver [about £500,000] the produce of the Trade at Nova Colonia . . . conveyed with the greatest secrecy not to give umbrage to the Court of Spain'.[5] Another estimate put the trade at this time at about £300,000 annually.[6]

The key role of Brazilian developments in the growth of English exports to Portugal was clearly recognized from the beginning by the English living in Portugal. In 1706 John Milner, the Lisbon Consul, wrote that the trade in English woollen manufactures 'improves

[1] See V. M. Godinho, *Annales* (1950), pp. 190-1.

[2] Letter of 19 February 1736, quoted by R. Southey, *History of Brazil* (1810-19), Vol. III, p. 294n.

[3] Lisbon Factory memorial, 6 June 1760, P.R.O. C.O. 388/53, LI.20.

[4] Walpole to Rochford, Attachment C, 4 July 1774, P.R.O. S.P. 89/77.

[5] Hay to Pitt, 29 August 1761, P.R.O. S.P. 89/54. The gold *crusado* was worth about 2s. 9d. and the silver *crusado* about 2s. 6d.

[6] Bougainville, *Voyage autour du Monde, 1766-1769*, quoted by R. C. Simonsen, op. cit., Vol. II, pp. 191-2n. Foreign manufactures, as well as being supplied to Brazil, were also shipped from Portugal to the Portuguese trading posts in Africa and in Asia. Such evidence as is available, however, suggests that these trades remained quite small and intermittent, showing no overall growth over the period to 1760. To a very substantial extent the Portuguese slave trade from Africa to Brazil was carried on directly from Brazil, and in small part depended on the re-export of European manufactures from Brazil to Africa. On the African slave trades, see C. R. Boxer, *The Golden Age of Brazil*, *passim*, and on the Asian trade, see H. Hallam Hipwell, 'The Portuguese East India Company, 1754-6', *Historical Association, Lisbon Branch, Report* (1941).

every day, and will doe more as their country grows richer which it must necessarily do if they can continue the importation of so much gold from the Rio every year'.[1] In 1711 the Lisbon Factory in one of its memorials considered that the last thirty years had seen a two-thirds increase in their woollen goods trade which 'does chiefly arise from the Improvement of the Portuguese Trade to the Braziles, and the great Quantity of Gold, that is brought from thence', and added 'as that trade does go on Encreasing our Woollen Trade will also probably Encrease proportionably'.[2] And in 1715 they tersely declared that the Brazil trade to and from Portugal was the 'Basis and Foundation' of their whole trade.[3] Subsequent English dispatches and memorials from Portugal reflect a continuing appreciation of Brazil's importance.[4]

Of the European manufacturing nations it is clear that England benefited most from the buoyancy of the Portuguese market. In 1716 the Lisbon Factory considered their trade to Brazil much exceeded the combined French and Dutch trades, and that British commodities in fact made up the 'chief part' of all trade to the colony.[5] And in 1729 an Englishman in Lisbon thought the value of exports from France, Holland and Hamburg to Portugal well below those of England: the French trade was put at some £165,000 annually, and that from Holland and Hamburg at £82,500 and £55,000 respectively, together with other combined exports from Holland, Hamburg and the Baltic countries worth £192,500 – while English exports to Portugal were put at £643,500.[6] The following year a French observer

[1] Milner to Hedges, 28 August 1706, P.R.O. S.P. 89/19.

[2] Memorial of 1 October 1711, P.R.O. C.O. 388/15, M.123.

[3] Memorial of 31 July 1715, P.R.O. C.O. 388/20, P. 71.

[4] In 1730 a French author referring to the 'immense' trades of other nations than the French with Portugal, pointed out that they 'augmentent à mesure que les Mines d'Or du Brézil deviennent plus considerables'. *Description de la Ville de Lisbonne*, p. 266.

[5] Memorial of 20 October 1716, P.R.O. C.O. 388/18, O.117.

[6] Attachment to Tyrawly to Newcastle, 26 June 1729, P.R.O. S.P. 89/35; B.N. Col. Pomb., Cod. 638, f. 461. Official English exports to Portugal in 1727-9 averaged £896,000 annually. C. Whitworth, op. cit., Part II, p. 27. A revision later in 1729 of the estimated value of English exports put them at £731,500, but did not consider the figures relating to other countries. Attachment to Compton to Newcastle, 6 August 1729 N.S., P.R.O. S.P. 89/35. The author of the earlier 1729 estimates had an interest in minimizing the English trade surplus with Portugal (and the consequent shipment of bullion to England) which may help to explain his low figure for English exports, and an interest in maximizing the trade surpluses with Portugal of other nations, which suggests a contrary bias concerning their exports.

remarked 'le Commerce des Anglois à Lisbonne est le plus considerable de tous; même selon bien des gens il y est aussi fort que celui des autres Nations ensemble'.[1] And in 1732 Lord Tyrawly, the English Envoy to Portugal, declared, perhaps with some exaggeration, 'the English are the Nation here of most Considerable Figure by far, both from our Numbers settled here, our Shipping and Trade'.[2] As English trade continued to grow, so its position would have become even more outstanding.

How did England come so to dominate the supply of manufactures to Portugal in this period, in spite of the competition of other manufacturing nations? It is unlikely that the Anglo-Portuguese commercial treaties of 1642, 1654, 1661 and the Methuen treaty of 1703 which regulated their mutual trade had much effect in this connection.[3] They set out the detailed legal and commercial guarantees essential if a trade carried on largely by Protestant merchants and involving much capital[4] was to flourish with an autocratic and Catholic country. But by and large similar privileges were enjoyed by other nations: in 1712 the English Consul in Lisbon pointed out, 'ours was the first treaty of Commerce & by subsequent treaties w:th France, Holland, Spain, Sweden, &c: they have granted the same priviledges to them as wee have'.[5] More important than the treaties in fact was the state of political relations between Portugal and other countries. During the War of the Spanish Succession, the French, the English merchants'

[1] *Description de la Ville de Lisbonne*, p. 224.

[2] Tyrawly to Newcastle, 6 June 1732, P.R.O. S.P. 89/37.

[3] For these treaties see V. M. Shillington and A. B. W. Chapman, op. cit., Part II, Chapters III and IV, and Sir Richard Lodge, 'The English Factory at Lisbon'. *Transactions of the Royal Historical Society* (1933), pp. 211-42.

[4] See below, Chapter 3.

[5] Milner to Lewes, 14 May 1712, P.R.O. S.P. 89/22. The Methuen treaty, it is true, had a particular importance for the English in restoring full legal recognition to the importation of English textiles, the trade in some of which had been hampered in the late seventeenth century by Portuguese import restrictions. But these pragmatical decrees had been falling into abeyance before the Methuen treaty was signed. V. M. Godinho, *Annales* (1950), p. 188. And other countries, it seems likely, were soon on a similar footing. In 1705, for example, the Portuguese signed a commercial treaty with the Dutch permitting Dutch cloths to enter freely. A. D. Francis, *The Methuens and Portugal, 1691-1708* (Cambridge, 1966), p. 211. In the case of France, the late seventeenth century commercial treaty had expressly stated that the French were to enjoy the same privileges as the English and other nations, and at Utrecht in 1713 the Portuguese treaty with France declared that commerce between the two countries was to be as formerly. M. E. Turner, 'Anglo-Portuguese Relations and the War of the Spanish Succession', pp. 18, 233.

principal competitors in Portugal, were seriously impeded in their trade with Portugal as a result of the very active Anglo-Portuguese alliance against France. During this crucial, commercially expansive first decade of the century in Portugal, French commerce fell away greatly which clearly favoured the sale of, and preference for, English wares.[1] French trade with Portugal was again seriously hampered during the later Anglo-French wars of the period to 1760, even though Portugal and France remained at peace, by the effects of English naval action.

English merchants also had certain economic advantages over their foreign competitors. The increasing Portuguese demand for manufactures came from peoples living in countries with warm climates, and was chiefly for light woollen and worsted textiles in the low to medium price range, suitable for their clothing and furnishing needs. At the end of the seventeenth century England was far more specialized in the production of such fabrics than either France, Holland or the German states, and consequently better placed to exploit an expanding market.[2] Moreover, the fall in English textile prices relative to the generally stable prices of Douro wines and Brazilian gold, Portugal's chief commercial returns to England, probably meant that the terms of trade between the two countries were moving in Portugal's favour from about 1715 to 1750, thus enabling her to purchase more English textiles than she would otherwise have been able to do. Further advantages came from the Portuguese wine trade to England. England provided the market for the great bulk of all Portuguese wines (and fruit) exported to European countries during these decades,[3] and the English merchants in Portugal controlled both the purchase and shipment of the wines sent to England.[4] Their extensive business connections with the wine producing and trading regions, particularly in the more populous northern provinces, greatly helped their business in imported manu-

[1] On the decline of French commerce with Portugal at the time, see *Description de la Ville de Lisbonne*, pp. 256-9.

[2] On the earlier decline of the Dutch worsted industry see C. Wilson, 'Cloth Production and International Competition in the Seventeenth Century', *Ec.H.R.*, 2nd series, Vol. XIII (1960), pp. 213-19.

[3] *Mercator's Letters on Portugal and its Commerce*, p. 18. See also the 1729 survey of Portuguese trade attached to Tyrawly to Newcastle, 26 June 1729, P.R.O. S.P. 89/35; B.N. Col. Pomb., Cod. 638, ff. 461-2.

[4] See below, Chapter 5.

factures. In 1758 some London Portugal merchants commented 'the Vintagers have always considered the English as their chief Benefactors and Support; and . . . the Trade of British Commodities at Oporto is intimately connected with and dependent upon That of the Wines',[1] while in 1759 an English merchant in Oporto remarked that the 'Woollen Business . . . is closely connected with the Wine Business'.[2]

English businessmen could probably also ship their goods to Portugal more cheaply than their principal competitors. The French, with their own wine production and colonial plantations, imported very little from Portugal, and while a substantial trade in sugar, tobacco and salt was carried on from Portugal with Amsterdam and Hamburg,[3] much less shipping space was probably required than in the very considerable wine trade with England. The likelihood of return cargoes from Portugal for English vessels was consequently greater than for French, Dutch or German vessels, which very probably made for lower freight charges for English exports. The advantage may have been even greater: in 1713 certain London merchants observed 'in times of peace ships have often carried out cargoes of goods freight free [to Portugal and Italy] only obliging the persons to lade them home with wines'.[4] Finally, a large and expanding trade with Portugal and her colonies, as with all the contemporary less-developed countries, demanded the ability to provide long credit and a plentiful supply of it. That this was so is clear from the credit commonly granted by English merchants with the textiles sold in Portugal: payment on sales for the metropolitan market was normally deferred about six months, while for the Brazil trade the period could extend to as much as two or three years; about 1758 the Portuguese indebtedness to England in relation to total

[1] Memorial of 12 July 1758, P.R.O. S.P. 89/51.

[2] Etty to Frankland, 5 May 1759, P.R.O. S.P. 89/51. In 1773 the Superintendent-General of Customs for northern Portugal rather bitterly wrote of Oporto as 'a city with an English heart where this Nation [the English] has much power and where nothing pleases except that which comes from England'. B.N. Col. Pomb., Cod. 691, f. 113.

[3] See *Mercator's Letters on Portugal and its Commerce*, pp. 11-15, and attachment to Tyrawly to Newcastle, 26 June 1729, P.R.O. S.P. 89/35; B.N. Col. Pomb., Cod. 638, ff. 461-2.

[4] *Cal. H. of L. MSS*. Vol. X (1712-14), p. 109. On this point see also R. Davis, 'Merchant Shipping in the Economy of the Late Seventeenth Century', *Ec.H.R.*, 2nd series, Vol. IX (1956), pp. 60-2.

exports, largely consisting of textiles, may have totalled about £1,500,000 annually.[1] The problem of capital supply may well have been the most serious factor handicapping French merchants. Lacking a single great commercial and financial centre they were unable to compete on equal terms with the English, who could draw on the concentrated mercantile wealth of London,[2] and also benefited from the chain of credit extending back into the manufacturing areas. The Dutch, on the other hand, suffered no such handicap, but the force of their financial bargaining power was much lessened by their limited manufacturing capacity.

Thus it seems clear that the secular growth of the Portuguese market together with England's strong competitive position among the European manufacturing nations principally account for the expansion of English exports to Portugal between 1700 and 1760 and the great bullion inflow into England. Certain other factors which favoured English trade are also noteworthy although their effect was more limited in time. Some contemporaries made much play with the 'prodigious' benefits flowing from the Methuen treaty of 1703, as have many later historians, but as noted above its real importance lay in putting the importation of English woollens back on a legal basis, and its actual stimulus to imports from England would have been only temporary. More important during the century's first decade were Portugal's imports of military supplies from England, including clothing and foodstuffs, as a consequence of the War of the Spanish Succession, in payment for which the English subsidies helped.[3] The supply of the English troops in Portugal and the English naval base at Lisbon entailed substantial shipments also.[4] It seems likely too that during the War of the Spanish

[1] See below, Chapter 3, pp. 59-60.

[2] See A. H. John, 'The London Assurance Company and the Marine Insurance Market of the Eighteenth Century', *Economica*, New Series, Vol. XXV (1958), pp. 135-6.

[3] During the war until 1711 England paid annually to Portugal a third of a million *crusados* (*c.* £42,000) and also the third of a million *crusados* subsidy the Austrian Emperor was committed to. England had also agreed to help maintain 13,000 Portuguese troops with their necessary arms and equipment, but did not altogether fulfil her obligations. See Miss M. E. Turner's thesis, 'Anglo-Portuguese Relations and the War of the Spanish Succession', pp. 90, 148, 158n.

[4] Much of this government trade was contracted out to merchants, and hence recorded by the Customs, but the shipments made directly by the Portuguese and English governments do not appear in the trade statistics. Much information on military supplies to Portugal in this war is contained in *Cal. Treas. Papers* 1702-7 and 1708-14, and *Cal. Treas. Books*, Vols. XVII-XXVII, *passim*.

Succession (and possibly in the later Anglo-Spanish wars) English trade benefited from the business carried on from Portugal with Spain, although there is some conflict of evidence on this: while one writer thought that not one per cent of the English goods shipped to Portugal went to Spain,[1] another considered 'a very great . . . contraband trade was carried on'.[2] Furthermore, during the three major Anglo-French wars of the period the disturbances English naval action caused to the supply of French West Indian sugar to Europe favoured the Brazilian sugar planters and hence English exports. In 1774 an Englishman in Lisbon remarked 'when England has a successful war with France the Brazil Sugars, Tobaccos and other commodities sell for near double the price than at other times; on such occasions [the Portuguese] are able to purchase British and other foreign Goods to a greater amount'.[3] This may have particularly applied during the Seven Years War, although the actual price increases were less than suggested, the average yearly price of Brazilian white sugar at Amsterdam rising from 0·23 guilders per pound in 1750-3 to 0·30 guilders in 1756-7 and 0·315 guilders in 1762-3.[4] English exports were also stimulated by the devastation caused by the earthquake at Lisbon in November 1755: according to one observer 'the gradual re-establishment of the Shops with their necessary assortments continued the demand [for woollens] for several years'.[5] These factors then would also have made some contribution to the expansion of Anglo-Portuguese trade in the years to 1760, and the last two mentioned, the accentuation of Brazilian and Portuguese prosperity during the Seven Years War and the Lisbon earthquake of 1755, would in particular have contributed to the peak levels of trade achieved in the later 1750s. It is not really clear why English exports to Portugal apparently remained broadly stable in the 1740s and early 1750s. In part this could have been due to the falling away of Portuguese wine shipments to England between 1745 and 1755, which would have reduced the Portuguese metropolitan capacity to purchase

1 *The British Merchant*, Vol. III, p. 98.

2 Campbell, quoted by A. T. Mahan, *The Influence of Sea Power upon History* (Boston, 1925), p. 228.

3 Walpole to Rochford, 4 July 1774, Attachment C, P.R.O. S.P. 89/77.

4 N. W. Posthumus, *Nederlandsche Prijsgeschiendenis* (Leiden, 1943), p. 123.

5 Walpole to Rochford, 4 July 1774, Attachment C, P.R.O. S.P. 89/77.

English exports:[1] it may also have been due to some slowing down in the rate of growth of Brazilian wealth. The deficiencies of the available English and Portuguese statistics, however, make discussion of this matter difficult to pursue.

[1] From an average value of £275,000 annually in the 1730s Portuguese wine shipments rose to £367,000 annually in 1741-5 and then fell back to £275,000 annually in 1746-50 and £230,000 in 1751-5. See Appendix V. English grain exports to Portugal also declined in the 1740s: wheat shipments, from an average value of £119,000 annually in the 1730s, fell to £59,000 annually in 1741-5, and averaged £90,000 annually between 1746 and 1755. See Appendix IV.

2 *Contraction in the 1760s*

IN THE 1760s the long period of expansion in Anglo-Portuguese commerce came to an end. As the expansiveness of the trade to 1760 had depended mainly on the buoyancy of Portuguese and Brazilian incomes, so did its decline in the 1760s spring essentially from the ending of this long period of prosperity.

During the 1760s English exports to Portugal sharply contracted: from an annual value of £1,301,000 in 1756-60 they fell away to £965,000 in 1761-5 and £595,000 in 1766-70. The yearly figures show that the decline began in 1762 and continued until the end of the decade. In the 1770s exports became more stable although with a tendency still to decline, averaging £613,000 annually in 1771-5 and £525,000 in 1776-80. Re-exports of foreign and colonial goods to Portugal underwent little change,[1] the contraction in business affecting English products and manufactures alone. The annual value of the principal textiles exported which had averaged over £1 million in the late 1750s slumped to £709,000 in 1761-5 and £459,000 in 1766-70, although in both periods they still accounted for over 70 per cent of total exports.[2] Woollen and worsted fabrics, especially the lighter and more moderately priced, remained most important, with bays still the leading single item, despite their fall to an annual export of £237,000 in 1766-70. Worsted stuffs came second, with shipments averaging £123,000 in these years. Shipments of the more expensive woollen cloths also decreased greatly, the combined value of short, long and Spanish cloths averaging only £53,000 annually by 1766-70. Worsted stocking and hat shipments fell away even more, the former to £20,000 annually in 1766-70, and the latter to £5,000. Of the other manufactures, wrought iron wares continued to stand out and in

[1] See Appendix II.
[2] See Appendix III.

contrast to the general tendency their trade increased.[1] Grain shipments to Portugal were substantial in the early 1760s: in 1761-5 wheat cargoes, still the principal item, averaged 90,000 quarters annually valued at £121,000, and accounted for 13 per cent of total exports. In 1766 a further 16,000 quarters of wheat went to Portugal, but thereafter the trade virtually ceased.

At the same time the trades to Portugal from Newfoundland and the mainland American colonies were growing. The end of English grain exports to Portugal encouraged corn importers there to turn more to other sources of supply, and this alone may explain the increasing imports from across the Atlantic. By 1769, according to the Lisbon Factory, the corn trade had become 'by far the most important branch' of the trade with the English colonies.[2] A survey based on information given by the English Consuls in Portugal indicates that annually in 1772-3 American wheat imports into Lisbon averaged 28,500 quarters valued at £47,250, while Indian corn imports averaged 13,570 quarters worth £12,200. Both were exceeded by flour shipments averaging 66,300 barrels valued at £79,200 while rice shipments averaged 24,000 quintals worth £8,900.[3] Imports of dried cod from Newfoundland and New England also apparently grew about this time: in 1772-3 Lisbon and Oporto's combined imports averaged 108,660 quintals worth £56,900.[4] Altogether, in 1772-3, Lisbon's imports from North America, which also included pipe and hogshead staves and other minor items, averaged £226,900 yearly (including freight charges averaging £45,000).

Recorded imports into England from Portugal, however, showed little change in the 1760s from their former level. Wines still predominated, accounting for over 80 per cent of total imports.[5] Exports from Portugal to English North America also changed little, salt and wines remaining the principal items. In 1769 the English Envoy

[1] To £29,000 annually by 1766-70.

[2] Memorial of 12 April 1769, f. 87, attached to Lyttelton to Weymouth, 6 May 1769, P.R.O. S.P. 89/68.

[3] 'An Account of . . . all Goods . . . imported into . . . Portugal from Great Britain and her Colonies' for 1772 and 1773. P.R.O. B.T. 6/62. Gaps in the survey unfortunately rule out a comprehensive estimate of American colonial trade to Portugal. A quintal was about one cwt.

[4] Ibid. In 1777 *bacalhau* imports into Lisbon, Oporto, Viana and Figueira came to 126,000 quintals worth 457,430 *milreis* (*c.* £123,600). *Arte e Diccionario do Commercio e Económia Portugueza* (Lisbon, 1784), p. 57.

[5] See Appendix V.

in Lisbon wrote that before the 1764 Act tightened up European trade with the colonies 'some of the English Merchants here were accustomed to send Wines to the Amount of 250 Pipes per Annum to the British Colonies' but that thereafter such trade had ceased.[1] By 1775, however, the English Consul in Lisbon considered a wine trade again customary, 'hardly any vessel . . . unless perhaps very lately' sailing without some casks, 'not perhaps exceeding thirty at the utmost'.[2] In 1773 fifty-three English or colonial-American vessels cleared Lisbon for North America, nineteen being bound for Newfoundland.[3]

The contraction in English exports caused a sharp fall in the official English trade surplus. From an annual average of over £1,000,000 in the late 1750s it declined to £650,000 in 1761-5 and to £239,000 in 1766-70, but the likely rise in textile prices at this time means that the official figures may exaggerate the real fall.[4] The English 'invisible' earnings without doubt substantially improved the English position,[5] so that on current account as a whole the actual surpluses were probably greater than the official surpluses. There is again no evidence of significant Portuguese payments through a third country, or of substantial English investment in fixed assets in Portugal, while the volume of English commercial capital in the country was probably falling with the decline in English trade, so that the surpluses continued to be regularly settled in bullion. Although bullion shipments on English trade account must have fallen away appreciably compared to earlier decades, this in part at least was compensated by the expanding North American colonial trades with Portugal whose large favourable balances for the most part were remitted initially to England.[6] Between 1761 and 1765 the annual London rate of exchange on Lisbon (average of the first rate quoted each month by Castaing), stood, as would be expected, below

[1] Lyttelton to Weymouth, 14 January 1769, P.R.O. S.P. 89/67. See also Lisbon Factory memorial, 24 July 1765, P.R.O. C.O. 388/95.

[2] Hort to Rochford, 12 February 1775, P.R.O. S.P. 89/79. In addition he thought 'large quantities of tea appear to have been carried [to America] clandestinely for a considerable time past, either as ballast or salt; and very recently some gunpowder, but so far . . . not a great deal, though several orders for it have arrived'. The latter, he remarked, 'is of a nature not now to be trifled with'.

[3] Walpole to Rochford, 4 July 1774, Enclosure N.2, P.R.O. S.P. 89/77.

[4] See below, 'Note on the use of the official English trade statistics', p. 140.

[5] See above, Chapter 1, pp. 19-20.

[6] On this, see Chapter 4.

gold export point (taken as 5s. 6d.), except for 1762 and 1763 when export rates ruled in a number of months. But between 1766 and 1770 the London rate fell to gold export point in four months only, in 1766. These were rather exceptional years, however: the London market price for gold was unusually high, the yearly price (average of the first price quoted each month by Castaing) ranging from £3. 19s. 0⅜d. per ounce in 1766 to £4. 0s. 2⅜d. in 1769, and bullion export points on the exchanges would have been higher too.[1]

As before, bullion was also shipped to England on the account of Dutch, German and other continental European merchants. The proportion of foreign merchants' shipments from Portugal which went first to England probably fell during the Seven Years War, when neutral warships were preferred to English warships because of the risk of attack by French privateers.[2] But it became very high afterwards. In 1767 it was observed that in times of peace between England and France the foreign merchants in Lisbon chose the English packet-boats to ship out their bullion 'because of their superior dispatch and [the] greater confidence' reposed on them,[3] and in 1769 the English Envoy in Lisbon could write 'the English Pacquet boats or other vessels employ'd in [the export of bullion] not only carry the Ballance due to British Subjects but also to those of France, Holland & other Countries of the North with which Portugal has any Trade'.[4] In this decade annual figures of the packets' cargoes are available—see Table III. These figures undoubtedly understate the total imports from Portugal, especially in wartime, due to the men-of-war and other shipping employed. Bearing in mind the declining size of the English trade surpluses and after allowing for the colonial-American remittances to England, the continuing great size of the packets' freights in these years suggests shipments on foreign merchants' accounts must have been quite noteworthy, possibly amounting to one-third of total imports at the end of the decade. Such an estimate is very uncertain, however;

[1] See Appendix VII.

[2] 'In time of war between Britain and France the [foreign] merchants [of Lisbon] use Dutch ships of war, or other neutrals, preferably to ours . . . because . . . neutral royal ships are not liable to the dangers of privateers.' *Occasional Thoughts on the Portuguese Trade* (1767), p. 11.

[3] Ibid.

[4] Attachment to Lyttelton to Weymouth, 21 June 1769, f. 48, P.R.O. S.P. 89/69.

it is also possible, in view of their declining interests, that English merchants were repatriating large sums of commercial capital from Portugal to England at this time.

Table III BULLION IMPORTED BY THE LISBON-FALMOUTH PACKET-BOATS, 1761-1769

	£		£
1761	548,532	1766	906,286
1762	286,099	1767	813,370
1763	693,676	1768	930,461
1764	1,186,714	1769	902,456
1765 (from 11 April)	631,081		

Source: B.N. Col. Pomb., Cod. 635, f. 445, Cod. 636, f. 10. (The faulty addition for 1763 and 1764 has been corrected.) The figures for 1765-9 are printed in V. Magalhães Godinho, *Prix et Monnaies au Portugal, 1750-1850* (Paris, 1955), p. 231.

Why did English exports to Portugal and bullion imports into England on English account contract so precipitately in the 1760s? The virtual ending of grain shipments after 1766 stemmed directly from the growth of English domestic demands for grainstuffs and the consequent rise in prices, which not only reduced the profitability of the trade but in some years led to a general prohibition on corn exports. On the other hand, the decline in the trade in manufactures very largely occurred because of the ending of the long period of Brazilian prosperity and the onset of a protracted depression in Portuguese trade which, according to its principal historian, Jorge de Macedo, reached its nadir in 1768-71 and remained serious until 1779.[1] The depression began with Portugal's unwilling entry into the Seven Years War in January 1762, when, as well as losing the benefits accruing to her as a neutral, her own commerce became subject to disturbance. The return of normal conditions in world sugar markets from 1764 further depressed the value of Brazilian output. From an average annual price of 0·315 guilders per pound in 1762-3 Brazilian white sugar on the Amsterdam market fell to 0·275

[1] For an account of the depression, see J. de Macedo, *A Situação Económica no Tempo de Pombal*, Chapter IV.

guilders in 1764-5.[1] Contemporary with this were more fundamental developments. Most serious was the beginning of an absolute decline in Brazil's gold output and trade. From the peak average of 14,600 kg annually in 1741-60 the output of the mines is estimated to have fallen to 10,350 kg in 1761-80,[2] while Professor Simonsen's figures suggest gold shipments to Portugal from being worth about £2,200,000 in 1760 had fallen back to about £750,000 in 1776.[3] This is supported by Magalhães Godinho's observation that the gold brought to Lisbon from Brazil had begun to diminish before 1765, and did so especially after that year.[4] These years also witnessed a marked slump in Brazil's sugar trade: her estimated exports of 2,500,000 *arrobas* in 1760 worth £2,380,000 had by 1770 fallen to 1,770,000 *arrobas*, and by 1776 to 1,500,000 *arrobas* worth £1,438,000.[5] Altogether, Brazil's total exports seem to have fallen from about £4,800,000 to about £3,000,000 between 1760 and 1776.[6] Further evidence of the slump in Brazilian trade can be seen in the profits earned by the Companhia do Grão Pará e Maranhão, which since its formation in 1755 had monopolized the Portuguese trade with northern Brazil: from the high levels of 1760-2 they subsequently fell away greatly and between 1767 and 1774 were negligible.[7] This depression in important sectors of Brazilian production and trade from about 1762 onwards markedly reduced the colony's effective demand for manufactures, causing a contraction in foreign imports from Portugal, including English products.

The decline in Brazil's prosperity also seriously depressed the incomes of the Portuguese Crown and the mercantile communities in Lisbon and Oporto. The yield of the *quinto*, the main tax levied on Brazilian gold production, fell away from an annual average of about 102 *arrobas* in 1751-60, to 97 in 1761-5, 86 in 1766-70 and 78 in 1771-5. Other branches of the royal revenue were similarly affected.[8] The

[1] N. W. Posthumus, op. cit., p. 123.

[2] A. Soetbeer, op. cit., p. 92, quoted by J. F. Normano, *Brazil. A Study of Economic Types*, p. 31.

[3] *Historia Economica do Brasil*, Vol. II, graph opposite p. 222.

[4] V. M. Godinho, *Annales* (1950), p. 195.

[5] R. C. Simonsen, op. cit., Vol. I, table opposite p. 170. See also J. de Macedo, *A Situação Económica no Tempo de Pombal*, pp. 169-70. An *arroba* was the Portuguese quarter.

[6] R. C. Simonsen, op. cit., Vol. II, graph opposite p. 222.

[7] J. de Macedo, *A Situação Económica no Tempo de Pombal*, p. 172.

[8] See ibid., Chapter IV.

depression can also be seen in the declining issue of *moedas de ouro* in Portugal: from an annual average value between 1752 and 1761 of 1,305,000 *milreis* it fell in 1762-70 to 1,004,000 *milreis*, and in 1771-82 to 569,000 *milreis*.[1] Falling Crown and mercantile incomes dampened purchasing power in Portugal, and so reduced the demand for foreign textiles as well as other products. The ending in 1762 of the hitherto large contraband trade conducted from Nova Colonia do Sacramento with Buenos Aires was a further blow. According to a Portuguese minister this 'was [in 1762] put a stop to by the Spaniards who had blockaded Nova Colonia . . . which occasioned a great diminution in the Remittances of Gold from the Rio de Janeiro, & in the consumption of English Goods'.[2] In 1773 the trade was still checked.[3] It is probable too that the terms of trade between England and Portugal were shifting in England's favour at this time with the rise in her textile prices. This movement may have begun in the 1750s but then Portugal's prosperity was still sufficiently expansive to more than absorb the English price increases: in the 1760s, however, the decline in Portuguese incomes would have made the depressing influence on imports from England more evident.

Whereas the Englishmen in Portugal had clearly recognized the prime significance of Brazilian developments for the expansion of English business to 1760, they failed on the whole (at least in their official correspondence) to appreciate their contrary significance in the 1760s. One exception, however, was an Englishman living in Lisbon, an 'able and intelligent person' in the Envoy's view, who in a letter written in 1774 displayed a considerable appreciation of what had been happening. He was aware 'that the principal Gold Mines have decreased in their produce, insomuch that the first Years after their discovery the annual remittances of Gold from the Brasils were from 20 to 23 millions of Cruzados [from about £2,857,000 to £3,286,000]; whereas of late Years it barely reaches to half that Sum'.[4] He further pointed out that the temporary stimulus to English

[1] Quoted by V. M. Godinho, *Prix et Monnaies au Portugal*, p. 255. In sterling these sums were about £353,000, £271,000 and £154,000 respectively.

[2] Attachment to Lyttelton to Shelburne, 1 September 1767, P.R.O. S.P. 89/63. See also attachment to Lyttelton to Weymouth, 21 June 1769, ff. 57-8, P.R.O. S.P. 89/69.

[3] Walpole to Rochford, 19 June 1773, P.R.O. S.P. 89/75.

[4] Walpole to Rochford, 4 July 1774, Attachment C, P.R.O. S.P. 89/77.

trade in the late 1750s and the beginning of the 1760s, given by the Lisbon earthquake and the wartime boost to Brazilian incomes, had been supplemented by the virtually complete destruction by fire in May 1764 of the Lisbon Custom House and its contents.[1] Two other factors contributory to the English trade decline were noted. First, the 'very considerable sums . . . annually paid since the Earthquake to Russia, Denmark, Sweden & Holland for Timber & Iron to rebuild the City [had] had a great Effect upon the sale of our Goods by drawing off . . . Money', and secondly, the 'establishment of the Royal Treasury in . . . 1762 had a great Effect on Trade in general; untill that time, the Revenue, laying in private hands, was frequently employed in Trade, whereas now . . . it is regularly carried into the Treasury'.[2]

In a long series of vigorous memorials to the English government the English factories in Portugal though essentially blamed the Portuguese government for their difficulties. They pointed out how a variety of Portuguese measures had harmed their trade and infringed their treaty rights, their aim being to obtain redress although in this they met with little success. Some of the actions of the Portuguese government at this time did adversely affect trade from England, such as the raising of import duties to finance Lisbon's rebuilding after the 1755 earthquake, which bore especially heavily when Portuguese incomes began falling, and the establishment of two companies in 1755 and 1759, the Companhia do Grão Pará e Maranhão and the Companhia de Pernambuco e Paraíba with exclusive trading rights to large areas of Brazil and with what proved to be rather restrictive trading policies.[3] Most serious, though, were the fresh attempts to develop domestic Portuguese industries, once again in response to the pressures of commercial depression. English trade in hats and silk goods clearly suffered from these ventures,[4] as probably did other products, although the policy was not in fact fully imple-

[1] The English Envoy reported soon after this event that 'the immediate Loss in effects is . . . about Five Hundred Thousand Pounds . . . His Majesty's Subjects are unhappily the greatest Sufferers. [They] had begun to Import their Goods for the Rio fleet . . . and most . . . were in the Custom House . . . to the Value of Two Hundred Thousand Pounds'. Hay to Halifax, 3 June 1764, P.R.O. S.P. 89/59.

[2] Walpole to Rochford, 4 July 1774, Attachment C, P.R.O. S.P. 89/77.

[3] See Lisbon Factory memorials, 6 June 1760 and 29 November 1764, P.R.O. C.O. 388/53, Ll. 20 and Ll. 24, No. 16, and memorial of 24 July 1765, C.O. 388/95, I.2.

[4] Lisbon Factory memorial, 24 July 1765, P.R.O. C.O. 388/95, I.2.

mented until 1769 and after.[1] The merchants in Lisbon also complained of a revival of French competition. In 1765 they reported the 'Crape Trade is entirely lost . . . owing to the French having introduced their Druggets', and that the French were importing large quantities of long ells and stuffs. The French had also introduced their long bays but until then with little success.[2]

From the early 1780s until the first years of the nineteenth century Portugal's commerce experienced a new phase of prosperity, resting largely on the development of trade with Asia and the re-export of Brazilian cotton to England.[3] English exports to Portugal, however, did not revive appreciably until the late 1790s, mainly because of the advances which had been made in Portuguese manufacturing industry, and for some years in this decade Portugal, officially at least, achieved a surplus in her visible trade with England. In 1808, following the French invasion of Portugal, occurred the end of an era in Anglo-Portuguese commercial relations, when Brazil, whose economic fortunes had been so influential for more than a century, was formally thrown open to direct trade from England.

[1] See J. de Macedo, *A Situação Económica no Tempo de Pombal*, Chapter V. The English merchants at Lisbon while recognizing that it would be 'unreasonable as to suppose that England has any right to complain of the establishment of Manufactories in Portugal, even where they interfere with those of our most Staple Commodities', thought, however, that the way in which British troops 'sent over for the defence of this Country in the late War' had been 'inveigled away from their duty . . . and are now employed in the Portuguese Woolen and other Manufactories . . . ungenerous to the last degree on the part of the Portuguese, for what is it less than stealing the sword that was drawn in their defence, and aiming it at the breast of their Protector?' Lisbon Factory memorial, 24 July 1765, P.R.O. C.O. 388/95, I.2.

[2] Ibid.

[3] V. M. Godinho, *Annales* (1950), p. 196. See also his study, *Prix et Monnaies au Portugal*, pp. 259-76.

COMMERCIAL ORGANIZATION

THE ORGANIZATION OF Anglo-Portuguese commerce between 1700 and 1770, including the trades between English North America and Portugal, is best examined by considering the four commodity-trades which together accounted for an overwhelming proportion of all the transactions. These were, first, the trade in English textiles to Portugal; second, the shipment of English and North American foodstuffs to Portugal; third, the import of Portuguese wine into England; and fourth, the transfer of bullion from Portugal to England. Between these branches of commerce there were significant differences in the factors which determine commercial organization – the physical and economic characteristics of the commodities themselves, the nature and distribution of their supply sources and markets, the degree of economic development in the countries concerned, and, not least of all, the policy of governments. The resulting contrasts in business practice warrant individual study of the constituent branches of trade.

3 *Textiles to Portugal and Brazil*

THE TEXTILES SHIPPED to Portugal between 1700 and 1770 were standardized and durable products, with a high value-to-bulk ratio and a generally widespread and popular market in both Portugal and Brazil.[1] Notable too in determining the organization of this trade was the comparative paucity of Portuguese mercantile capital. In 1730 a French observer thought the Portuguese merchants 'tout à fait bornés dans leur Commerce. La plupart ne [savent] point ce que c'est que de faire venir les Marchandises de leur source, ils se contentent de les acheter à Lisbonne';[2] and in 1765 the Lisbon Factory considered the 'trade here is carried on chiefly by the long Credit given by Foreigners to the Natives, who have seldom large Capitals'.[3] Politically, the trade was liberally regulated. Since 1606, with the collapse of the chartered Company of Merchants trading to Spain and Portugal, commerce with Portugal had been open to all, while by 1721 virtually all English export duties had been abolished. Furthermore, the commercial treaties between the two countries provided a satisfactory

[1] In 1730 a Frenchman writing on Lisbon remarked that the great sale of English bays in the city 'vient de ce que les Portugais sont dans l'usage de s'en servir pour les habillemens de deuïl, & de ce que les Femmes des Artisans s'en font communément des habits: à quoi il faut ajouter que les Hommes de toute condition usent des Robes de chambre dont le dessus & le dessous sont aussi de cette Etoffe'. *Description de la Ville de Lisbonne*, pp. 225-6. In 1772, according to the English Envoy in Lisbon, English bays were 'the chief Wear . . . of all Classes from the highest to the lowest, and are what the Cloakes are made of, which [are] the constant wear of the Country allmost all the Year'. Walpole to Rochford, 15 April 1772, P.R.O. S.P. 89/72. Cf. also Mathew Decker's observation that 'a great Part of the [? English] Woollens sold in Portugal is for the Brazils, and the great Consumption of Woollens in the Brazils is by the Negroes'. *An Essay on the Causes of the Decline of the Foreign Trade* (1744), p. 107.

[2] *Description de la Ville de Lisbonne*, pp. 229-30.

[3] Memorial of 24 July 1765, P.R.O. C.O. 388/95, I.2. 'The Subjects of Portugal have not funds of their own sufficient to carry on their Trade upon their own Accounts. The Foreign Merchants are obliged to give them Credit, and sometimes long Credit.' Hay to Egremont, 18 March 1763, P.R.O. S.P. 89/58. See also *Mercator's Letters on Portugal and its Commerce*, pp. 4-5.

legal and fiscal basis for business.[1] In general the merchants in London, who dominated the trade for most of the period, did not face especially difficult business problems. Their chief ones were similar to those in the other branches of trade with the less-developed countries – how to finance the long-term investment often necessary, the vexed question of finding efficient and reliable factors to handle consignments, and how returns could best be made for their goods. In fact, the expansiveness of the trade, together with its liberal regulation and the proximity of Portugal, must have made it one of the most attractive outlets for English exporters at this time.

The geographical pattern of the trade was simple. The low freight costs, non-perishability, and variety of the commodities, facilitated and encouraged the use of entrepôts and the concentration of trade on them. Throughout the period to 1770 the textiles exported were overwhelmingly shipped from London.[2] In the case of bays and worsted stuffs, however, there was some growth of outport shipments after the Seven Years War: of the bays worth £237,000 annually exported between 1766 and 1770 some 23 per cent went out from the outports. The other case of note relates to perpetuanas and serges: until their decline after 1724 about one-third of their exports were shipped from the provincial ports, very largely from Exeter.[3] The importance of the Portuguese ports can be shown only approximately owing to the paucity of statistics. Undoubtedly though most business by far was with Lisbon and Oporto alone. Lisbon was not only a major market in itself, but was the leading entrepôt for the Tagus region and much of southern Portugal, as well as the principal centre for Portuguese colonial commerce. Oporto was the leading port of northern Portugal, serving the prosperous and populous Douro and Minho provinces, and it also had interests in the colonial trades. A survey of 1729[4] suggests that Lisbon then absorbed some 65 per cent

[1] On this see, Sir Richard Lodge, 'The English Factory at Lisbon'. *Transactions of the Royal Historical Society* (1933), pp. 211-24. In 1713 three leading Portugal merchants told the Commissioners for Trade that the treaties 'provided very well' for English trade. *Journal of Trade*, 1708/9-1714/5, p. 483.

[2] This statement, and those following, are based on P.R.O. Customs 3.

[3] See W. G. Hoskins, *Industry, Trade and People in Exeter, 1688-1800* (Manchester, 1935), p. 67.

[4] Attached to Compton to Newcastle, 6 August 1729 N.S., P.R.O. S.P. 89/35. This survey revised an earlier one of Anglo-Portuguese trade and on this question seems more realistic. The earlier survey is found in B.N. Col. Pomb., Cod. 638, ff. 461-2, and in the P.R.O. attached to Tyrawly to Newcastle, 26 June 1729, S.P. 89/35.

of all English exports and Oporto about 25 per cent. Since the ratios of Lisbon's and Oporto's imports of textiles and foodstuffs were probably about the same, these percentages would roughly indicate their importance in the textile trade relative to each other, but it probably rather overstates their combined importance relative to the other Portuguese ports. The 1729 survey further mentions only Figueira, which served Coimbra, and Viana as also taking imports from England, but small textile shipments would also have been made to the lesser Portuguese ports, Aveiro, Caminha, Setubal and Faro. Between 1730 and 1760 Lisbon's leading position very probably became even greater with the growth of the Brazilian market.

Throughout the years to 1770 the large capital needs of this export trade meant that merchants in England would dominate its conduct and finance. And the concentrated mercantile wealth of London and its advantages as an entrepôt meant that its merchants would have the leading role.[1] The 'Portugal Merchants' of London consigned goods to factors or correspondents in Portugal who arranged their sale for a commission. London merchants also financed shipments from provincial ports.[2] The extent to which merchants specialized on the Portugal trade is not clear: undoubtedly some did, such as William Braund,[3] while others traded more widely to include Spain and markets in the Mediterranean. Throughout the period, according to the names of signatories of a number of memorials on the trade, a majority of the London Portugal merchants had Anglo-Saxon or British names.[4] But merchants of foreign, especially French and Dutch descent, were also well represented, while, although Jewish names appear rarely, part of the trade was carried on by Jews, often Sephardic in origin, such as Benjamin Mendes da Costa in the mid-1720s.[5]

[1] Some clothiers made shipments to Portugal on their own account, employing merchants in London and elsewhere as agents; but there is no evidence to suggest that this did not remain an overwhelmingly merchant-dominated trade.

[2] In 1724 following a dispute over bullion remittances from Portugal some London merchants complained they could not have 'their Cash at their Command in Cornwall or Devon, where they often want it, to lay out in [local] Woollen Manufactures'. 'Case of the Portugal Merchants' [20 August 1724], P.R.O. S.P. 100/39.

[3] L. S. Sutherland, *A London Merchant*, Chapter II.

[4] See, for example, memorials of 6 June 1711 (16 names), P.R.O. C.O. 389/22, f. 194; 21 August 1716 (34 names), P.R.O. C.O. 388/18, O.108; 17 May 1727 (53 names), P.R.O. S.P. 100/39, f. 187; [May] 1756 (63 names), P.R.O. C.O. 388/47, f. 16; and 27 December 1759 (59 names), P.R.O. S.P. 89/52.

[5] Born in France in 1697 he lived in Amsterdam from 1700 until 1724 when he moved to London. P.R.O. S.P. 100/39, f. 182.

In 1732 the English Envoy in Portugal wrote that 'the greatest Dealers . . . in our Woollen Goods are the Jews in London',[1] but this certainly exaggerated the true position. Portuguese nationals in London trading to Portugal were few and far between: in 1738 'very few' Portuguese merchants were in London.[2] They included Miguel Vianna, who in the early 1720s had lived in London for about thirty years and had 'all along carried on a trade to most parts of Europe but chiefly to Portugall where I sent sundry woollen goods',[3] and Manoel Dias Santos who had debts outstanding in Lisbon of above £20,000 in 1755.[4]

Unfortunately records illuminating the London end of this trade are extremely rare. Miss Sutherland's study of William Braund is therefore of particular interest. Between 1741 and 1756 Braund made many shipments to Lisbon. He kept no stock or warehouse but when he thought fit purchased goods from specialized suppliers. These included the London merchants, Samuel and Thomas Fludyer, Brice Fisher, the Blackwell-Hall factor, who met his broadcloth needs, and Jeremiah, John and Robert Royd who supplied shalloons; and provincial men, such as Thomas Ruggles of Bocking, Essex, who supplied almost all his long bays. The purchases were put out for dyeing and finishing where necessary, and a specialized packer, Thomas Burfoot, was employed who also arranged their shipment. The 'sheer mobility and poise' of the purely intermediary position occupied by Braund has been well stressed by Miss Sutherland.[5] A surviving business ledger belonging to Robert Wilmot, a London merchant who between 1708 and 1714 shipped textiles in quantity to Lisbon and Oporto as well as to Spain, bears out Miss Sutherland's point. Wilmot also kept no stock but bought his goods from suppliers and employed others for such dyeing and finishing as was necessary.[6] Regrettably neither Braund's nor Wilmot's accounts give details of the credit obtained from suppliers. The only evidence found on this point concerns the supply of West Riding and Westmorland cloths to a London merchant. In March 1739 Walter Stanhope of Leeds offered

[1] Tyrawly to Newcastle, 23 May 1732, P.R.O. S.P. 89/37. See also Castres to Amyand, 26 June 1753, P.R.O. S.P. 89/48.

[2] Tyrawly to Newcastle, 14 February 1738, P.R.O. S.P. 89/40.

[3] P.R.O. S.P. 89/90, f. 102.

[4] Memorial of Charles Eastgate and others, May 1765, P.R.O. S.P. 89/60.

[5] L. S. Sutherland, op. cit., pp. 18-19, 26-9.

[6] O.F. (Lond.). Robert Wilmot's Ledger.

to supply cloth to the merchant's order and suggested the best arrangement for payment would be 'if you will order any friend in London to accept my drafts at three months date upon receipt of bill of lading from Hull'.[1] And in July 1740 Joshua Curtis of Kendal reported the dispatch to London of woollen masquerades and other cloths for which he was drawing a bill payable at 28 days.[2] It seems likely that the credit extended by suppliers was usually short, and that the London exporter got little assistance from this direction in the finance of his trade.

The problem of securing satisfactory service from factors in Portugal could be tackled in a number of ways. A branch of the firm could be established there, firms with family connections could be employed, as by William Braund between 1743 and 1763,[3] or factors could be selected who were willing and wealthy enough to import from England on their own account and who in turn employed and depended upon the London merchant as an agent. Where the London merchant imported Portuguese commodities on his own account, as did Robert Wilmot, the promise of his orders no doubt encouraged attention in the disposal of consignments.[4] As well as English factors much use was made in Lisbon of Dutch, German and Italian houses, as well as Portuguese. Between 1741 and 1743 William Braund's agents were the Dutch firm of Schutte, Buess and Renner,[5] while sometime in the early 1720s Miguel Vianna declared that he had employed 'divers Houses at Lisbon as well as English . . . Portuguese, Dutch and Hamburghers'.[6] And in 1728 Benjamin Mendes da Costa's correspondents were Bervardi and Medici.[7] On the whole this practice was most prevalent before 1721, when the English consular levies on imports for charitable purposes applied to consignments to English but not foreign houses.[8]

[1] P.R.O. C.M.E. C.110, 19, 20, Pratt *ex parte*, Stanhope to Hitchcock, 3 March 1738-9.

[2] Ibid., Curtis to Hitchcock, 19 July 1740.

[3] Braund's nephew, Benjamin Branfill, was a partner in the firm of Jackson, Branfill and Goddard, his Lisbon agents. L. S. Sutherland, op. cit., p. 24.

[4] Wilmot's factors in Lisbon and Oporto, James and Samuel Garnier and Dowker and Stuckey respectively, both shipped wines to his order. O.F. (Lond.). Robert Wilmot's Ledger.

[5] L. S. Sutherland, op. cit., p. 24.

[6] P.R.O. S.P. 89/90, f. 102.

[7] P.R.O. S.P. 100/39, f. 182.

[8] See Lisbon Factory memorial, 1 October 1711, P.R.O. C.O. 388/15 M.123, and A. R. Walford, *The British Factory in Lisbon*, pp. 33-6.

On their arrival in Lisbon and Oporto the goods were sold to local and provincial shopkeepers and dealers, and to merchants trading to the colonies. Marked differences existed in the credit extended to purchasers. In the local trades, with their fairly rapid turnover, it only occasionally went beyond six months. In 1701 two months' credit for sales to shopkeepers in Lisbon and from the surrounding countryside was noted as common,[1] while in January 1740 an Oporto cloth factor wrote of the sale of a consignment of bays and stuffs to be paid 'half or thereabouts now in the fair of Arrifana, and the remainder in a few months'.[2] Terms, however, could be extended by unpunctuality in payment, a practice an English visitor to Lisbon in 1701 apparently regarded as common when he wrote 'three months after ye sale ye Merch^t^ goes to ye Shopkeeper & perhaps makes a shift to get in ye debt in 7 or 8 months'.[3]

On the other hand turnover in the Portuguese trade to Brazil was markedly slower. The *frota* system, in force until 1765, confining all trade to and from the colony to four fleets sailing annually between Lisbon and Rio de Janeiro, Bahia, Pernambuco and Grão Pará and Maranhão, distinctly slowed business. Moreover, delays to the departure of fleets and in their return were not unknown, while sometimes particular fleets sailed only biennially or even triennially.[4] The great distances involved in internal Brazilian trade, the remoteness of the mining settlements, and the poor communications, also meant that goods shipped there were usually sold on credit and often long credit.[5] Long-term investment was consequently inherent in Portuguese colonial trade. The credit actually given by the factors varied. Goods might be sold to be paid for on the arrival of the next fleet from one of the Brazilian ports: in September 1758, for instance, John White of Lisbon sold goods valued at 2000 *milreis* (about £540)

[1] B.M. Add. MSS. 23,726, ff. 20-1.

[2] P.R.O. C.M.E. C.110, 19, 20, Pratt *ex parte*, Hitchcock to Hitchcock, 6 November 1740.

[3] B.M. Add. MSS. 23,726, f. 21.

[4] On the *frotas* see, V. M. Godinho, *Annales* (1950), pp. 191-2. On the delays see Hay to Conway, 21 September 1765, P.R.O. S.P. 89/60, and attachment to Lyttelton to Weymouth, ff. 57-8, 21 June 1769, P.R.O. S.P. 89/69.

[5] 'At the time of [the fleet's] arrival at the Rio Janeiro there us'd to be a kind of Fair held, like that of Portobello, to which the People from the Mines resorted in great numbers, paid their old debts and took up large quantities of Goods upon fresh Credit.' Attachment to Lyttelton to Weymouth, ff. 57-8, 21 June 1769, P.R.O. S.P. 89/69. See also Lisbon Factory memorial, 6 June 1760, P.R.O. C.O. 388/53, Ll. 20.

to Manoel da Silva Fonseca who agreed to pay on 'the arrival of the first fleet that comes to this city from Pernambuco'.[1] More often payment was arranged for the return of the fleet on which the goods were consigned,[2] which usually meant at least a year, or longer if the fleet was delayed. But to a considerable extent payments were deferred for two or three years until the proceeds of the sales in Brazil were remitted to Lisbon. In 1760 the Lisbon Factory declared that agreements to pay on the fleets' return were 'seldom complied with, and the foreign merchant is satisfied with receiving half or even a third of his debt by the first fleet, and does not think it very bad pay if he receives the whole at the return of the third fleet'.[3] In the same year the Envoy in Lisbon remarked that the 'British Merchants give a Credit of two or three years to the Portuguese Merchants trading to the Brazil. This Credit was . . . founded in necessity because the Portuguese Merchants could only be enabled by their Returns from Brazil to pay for the Goods which they purchase from the British Merchants.'[4]

As a result, the English capital annually tied up in the textile trade with Portugal (including that involved in the business of the English firms in Portugal which is discussed below), must have been very considerable, its actual size at any time depending on the current level of trade. No estimates of the sums involved have survived, but there are two estimates of the investment in Portugal relating to all English exports. In 1729 an English merchant in Lisbon thought 'on a very moderate computation' that the English constantly had an investment in Portugal consisting of goods unsold and debts outstanding of 2,500,000 *milreis* (about £675,000) or upwards,[5] which was probably well below the actual amount. And in 1758 certain London merchants thought that the Portuguese were never indebted to England less than 'the full amount of above Two Years Importations' from

[1] T. de T., F.F., Conserv. Ingles, Maço VII, White *v.* Fonseca, f. 4.

[2] Memorial of Lisbon Factory, 24 May 1760, printed in *Memorials of the British Consul and Factory at Lisbon* (1766), pp. 42-3.

[3] Ibid.

[4] Kinnoul to Pitt, 7 June 1760, P.R.O. C.O. 388/53, Ll. 23. See also Kinnoul to Pitt, 14 April 1760, P.R.O. Chatham MSS. Vol. 94, ff. 85-6. In 1701 the returns of the Brazil trades to Lisbon were made '½ in 16m[onths] ye other ½ drippling', according to an English visitor to the city. B.M. Add. MSS. 23, 72b, f.23.

[5] Attachment to Tyrawly to Newcastle, 26 June 1729, P.R.O. S.P. 89/35; B.N. Col. Pomb. Cod., 638, ff. 461-2.

England,[1] at that time implying a sum in the region of £2,500,000, although £1,500,000 was probably nearer the mark.[2]

The London merchants therefore faced two distinct markets which tied up their capital for different periods. As would be expected the gross profits earned were more or less commensurate with the period involved. In 1769 it was said in Lisbon that the merchants made 'from seven to ten per Cent. upon the Goods they sell in this City, from fifteen to seventeen upon those they dispose of to Shopkeepers in the Country & from twenty-five to thirty per Cent. upon those they sell to be sent to Brazil'.[3] And in 1760 the Lisbon Factory estimated their average profit on sales to the Portuguese merchants at 12 to 15 per cent.[4] The prime consideration determining how merchants instructed factors to dispose of consignments was probably the size of their trading capitals. The lesser men probably concentrated on the metropolitan trades requiring their factors to ensure payment within a limited time. This may have been the case in 1739 when a merchant named White emphasized that he must have his 'returns' for a consignment to Oporto within twelve months.[5] While the wealthier men left it to their factors to sell on 'the best terms' possible.

In the early years of the century, as they were entitled to do by treaty, the Lisbon factors, on behalf of their principals, themselves shipped goods to Brazil although never to any great extent. In 1716 such transactions by English merchants as a whole were thought to average £30-40,000 annually.[6] As well as offering a further profit, shipment to Brazil solved the problem of goods that sold slowly in Lisbon.[7] Until about 1720 this activity was encouraged by the existence of a handful of English business houses there: in 1716 there were four such houses, three in Bahia and one in Rio de Janeiro.[8] Subsequently the number

[1] Memorial of London Portugal merchants 12 July 1758, P.R.O. S.P. 89/51.

[2] An estimate of 1759 of the total English capital 'lying in Portugal', which would have included the large sums associated with the wine trade, put it at between 3 and 4 million sterling. Grosett to Wood, 9 May 1759, P.R.O. S.P. 89/51. Grosett signed a London Portugal merchants' memorial of December 1759. P.R.O. S.P. 89/52.

[3] Lyttelton to Weymouth, 14 January 1769, P.R.O. S.P. 89/67.

[4] Lisbon Factory memorial, 6 June 1760, P.R.O. C.O. 388/53, Ll. 20.

[5] B.M. Add. MSS. 22,857, f. 17.

[6] *Journal of Trade*, 1714/5-1718, p. 180.

[7] Cf. Miguel Vianna's remarks in the mid-1720s concerning woollens consigned to Lisbon. 'As all [the] goods could not be disposed of at Lisbon I order'd my Correspondents there to ship them on my account for the Rio de Janeiro.' P.R.O. S.P. 89/90, f. 102.

[8] Lisbon Factory memorial, 20 October 1716, P.R.O. C.O. 388/18, O. 177.

fell[1] and the need to employ Portuguese factors in Brazil proved a serious discouragement.[2] With the founding of the monopolistic Companhia do Grão Pará e Maranhão and the Companhia de Pernambuco e Paraíba, in 1755 and 1759, direct English trade to these regions was prevented, but by then it was unimportant.[3]

The Portuguese paid their debts almost invariably in cash or local bills of exchange. But occasionally the factors in Lisbon were obliged to accept payments in colonial products.[4] Before remitting the balances to England the factor deducted any expenses he had incurred, freight payments, import duties, and consulage as well as his commission. Remittances could take the form of local products, amongst which wines were outstanding. But most exporters did not import wines, textile merchants and wine importers in England constituting broadly distinct groups. Thus in the main exporters received their returns in either bills of exchange or in bullion.[5]

Throughout the period the English houses in Lisbon and Oporto commonly combined their business as factors with one on their own account, employing London and provincial firms to supply goods to their order. For instance, in 1727 George Clarke of Oporto was employing Joseph and John Veale of Exeter to ship him woollen goods,[6] while in the early 1750s Daniel Hoissard of Lisbon had been supplied with goods for many years by Minyer and Hamerton of London.[7] Joint ventures were also undertaken with merchants in England. In 1709 Benjamin Chaplin of Lisbon had a two-thirds and one-half interest respectively in shipments of Colchester bays and silk hose made him by Robert Wilmot.[8] From 1755 the share of the trade conducted by the English firms in Portugal increased notably. In

[1] Lumley to Carteret, 3 February 1723 N.S., P.R.O. S.P. 89/30.

[2] The disadvantages, principally of a legal nature, are set out in the London Portugal merchants' memorial, 21 August 1716, P.R.O. C.O. 388/18, O.108.

[3] Kinnoul to Pitt, 14 April 1760, P.R.O. Chatham MSS. Vol. 94, f. 87; memorial of 12 April 1769, f. 102, attached to Lyttelton to Weymouth, 6 May 1769, P.R.O. S.P. 89/68.

[4] In 1752 some London Portugal merchants remarked that they were sometimes obliged to take sugar in payment for woollen goods. *Journal of Trade*, 1750-3, p. 275. See also L. S. Sutherland, *A London Merchant*, p. 34n., and memorial of 12 April 1769, attached to Lyttelton to Weymouth, 6 May 1769, P.R.O. S.P. 89/68.

[5] This is discussed further in Chapter 7.

[6] P.R.O. C.O. 388/91, A.67.

[7] See their petition to Henry Fox, 24 December 1755, P.R.O. S.P. 89/50.

[8] O.F. (Lond.). Robert Wilmot's Ledger, f. 33.

1758 the Consul in Lisbon even considered the 'greatest part' was on their account,[1] while in 1769 the Envoy thought the English in Lisbon 'were formerly almost all Factors' but that 'at present almost every man in the Factory is a Merchant and not a Factor'.[2] Bearing in mind the boom in textile shipments during the Seven Years War and the huge investment this necessitated, these views certainly underestimate the London merchants' continuing role. Nevertheless, the share of the firms in Portugal did increase. This no doubt arose in part out of their growing wealth after half a century of commercial expansion, but it reflected in the main a growing reluctance on the part of London merchants to trade so extensively to Portugal. This reluctance stemmed initially from the Lisbon earthquake of 1755 in which many suffered heavy losses,[3] and which for some time produced great uncertainty about payments. It was reinforced by the nationalist economic policies pursued by Pombal in these years. The effect was that the houses in Portugal were obliged to increase their own imports to maintain their business and incomes.[4]

Some increase occurred too towards the end of the period in the Portuguese share of the trade. Some importing by Portuguese houses had all along been practised, but in 1759 it was observed in Oporto that 'almost all the Portug^{ze} who are . . . of any Substance import their own [woollen] Goods and are falling into it daily more and more'.[5] Although in such a year, with England at war and Portugal neutral, a temporary increase in the Portuguese share of the trade was to be expected, nevertheless it does seem to have grown secularly. The Brazil trading companies created in the late 1750s by Pombal imported part of their needs,[6] and by 1774 according to the English Consul in Lisbon, Portuguese names on cargo manifests had grown to a considerable number, whereas until 'late years' they had hardly appeared.[7] A leading Oporto merchant at this time was Antonio Ribeira de Faria, whose debts in England in 1773 included £11,000 to Pemberton and Milnes of Wakefield and £8,445 to Hyer and Barclay

[1] Frankland to Pitt, 20 August 1758, P.R.O. S.P. 89/51.

[2] Attachment to Lyttelton to Weymouth, 21 June 1769, f. 56, P.R.O. S.P. 89/69.

[3] See the memorial of sixty-three London Portugal merchants, 15 May 1756, printed by Miss Sutherland, *A London Merchant*, Appendix III.

[4] Attachment to Lyttelton to Weymouth, 21 June 1769, f. 56, P.R.O. S.P. 89/69.

[5] Etty to Frankland, 5 May 1759, P.R.O. S.P. 89/51.

[6] Attachment to Lyttelton to Weymouth, 21 June 1769, f. 26, P.R.O. S.P. 89/69.

[7] Hort to Rochford, 8 September 1774, P.R.O. S.P. 89/77.

of London.[1] Despite the growth of Portuguese interests, however, it is clear that this trade remained overwhelmingly in the hands of English merchants.

[1] Walpole to Rochford, 22 September 1773, P.R.O. S.P. 89/75.

4 *Foodstuffs to Portugal*

THE ENGLISH AND North American grainstuffs and the North American cod shipped to Portugal, like the English textiles, found a popular market in the country at large, especially in the towns. Their trade too was favourably regarded by both English and Portuguese governments: since 1688 English grain exporters could claim a bounty of five shillings for each quarter of wheat exported and smaller sums for other grains, while Portugal's dependence on foreign foodstuffs meant that little or no duties were placed on imports.[1] But in other respects there were significant differences from the textile trade. In the first place, grainstuffs and fish were much more perishable, being liable to 'heating' in transit,[2] and incapable of long storage in Portugal's southern climate.[3] And second, their supply prices and market prices in Portugal were also more unstable, owing primarily to the variations that occurred in harvest yields in Portugal and in England, North America and the other countries supplying grain to Portugal,[4] and to variations in the output of the fisheries.[5] Merchants consequently faced much greater risk and uncertainty in these trades and this affected their business practice.

[1] *Os Privilegios do Inglez nos Reynos e Dominios de Portugal* (1736), p. 79 et seq.

[2] Corn, flour and fish were classed by John Weskett among the 'most hazardous' subjects of insurance in respect of damage liable in sea transit. *A Complete Digest of the Theory, Laws and Practice of Insurance* (1781), p. 106.

[3] 'Corn being by its nature a very perishable commodity, this hot Climate soon destroys it.' Lisbon Factory memorial, 24 July 1765, P.R.O. C.O. 388/95, I.2. Cf. 'English [grain] is not so fit for keeping [at Lisbon] as Streights grain', i.e. that coming from the Mediterranean. *Mercator's Letters on Portugal and its Commerce* (1754), p. 54.

[4] About 1765 the Portuguese generally received their largest supplies of grainstuffs 'from England and its Colonies and the different Ports of the Mediterranean: some little comes from Holland, Danzig & Spain [and] when wheat is cheap in France and the exportation allowed, they pour in very large supplies'. Lisbon Factory memorial, 24 July 1765, P.R.O. C.O. 388/95, I.2.

[5] On the instability of grain prices, see Chapter 8, p. 111, and of cod prices, see below, p. 74.

From 1700 until 1766 London was by far the leading English grain export port, although its position was never as commanding as in the textile trade. The bulkiness of the product, and the consequent greater significance of freight costs, coupled with its perishability encouraged direct shipment from the provincial ports whose hinterlands yielded corn surpluses for export. In the first period, 1702-8, when wheat exports to Portugal were considerable (taken as 20,000 quarters or more annually) the outports' share of the average shipment of some 77,000 quarters annually was about 25 per cent.[1] The lowness of this figure is probably explained by the great hazards that direct shipments from the east coast ports faced in these war years, the London trade benefiting from the centring of the convoys organized for Portugal on the Thames. The next period of considerable exports, 1711-16, saw shipments from the outports accounting for 35 per cent of the total, while in 1721-4 and 1730-9 they made up as much as 65 and 55 per cent respectively. The remaining periods, 1742-55 and 1759-1766, again included years when England was at war with France and Spain, and the outports' share fell back to 50 and 40 per cent respectively.

The paucity of Portuguese statistics rules out close examination of the position of the Portuguese ports. But the 1729 survey of Anglo-Portuguese commerce which put Lisbon's and Oporto's share of total English exports at 65 and 25 per cent respectively,[2] probably fairly indicates their importance relative to each other in the grain trade, although it is likely that it exaggerates their combined position relative to other ports. The additional costs and risks involved in coastal transhipment would have encouraged as direct a supply to Portuguese markets as possible, so that the lesser ports in aggregate would have handled more than 10 per cent of the trade.

The grain trade was largely in the hands of London and provincial merchants, who employed factors in Portugal on a commission basis to dispose of their consignments. As in the textiles trade, the exporter generally kept no stock, but bought as necessary from specialist factors. These factors, at least in London, often looked after the

[1] This calculation and those following are based on P.R.O. Customs 3. 1705, 1712 and 1727 are not included since the ledgers are missing for these years.

[2] Attachment to Tyrawly to Newcastle, 26 June 1729, P.R.O. S.P. 89/35; B.N. Col. Pomb., Cod. 638, ff. 461-2.

shipping of consignments as well. Customs statements of the grain loaded for Portugal in London between January 1764 and February 1766,[1] show that this business was highly concentrated. Of the total loading of wheat (by far the most important item) of 121,622 quarters, made up of 261 separate ladings, 68 per cent was entered in the names of three men alone, Thomas Farrer, John Thompson and James Rondeau, out of the thirty-nine altogether involved.[2] Farrer was outstanding: he made eighty-three separate ladings in these years comprising 42 per cent of the total trade.

Grain exporters were far more flexible in their business than the textile exporters.[3] Consignments were sent out more irregularly and more opportunistically, whenever prices at home and in Portugal seemed encouraging. This can be seen in the quite different seasonal patterns of the two trades, as discussed in Chapter 8. The instructions given to the masters of vessels carrying grain too were often more open, less precise. Instead of indicating delivery to a factor in a particular port, exporters would instruct masters to call in at certain ports to ascertain whether the cargo should be unloaded there or carried further where prices were more attractive. Lisbon was frequently designated in this way since as well as being a great market it was also a major centre of commercial intelligence for the other Portuguese ports and for Spain and southern Europe.[4] Such discretionary instructions can be seen in a memorial of Fenwick and Blakestow of Berwick who in (?) early 1764 loaded two ships, the *Charming Jenny* and the *Mary*, with wheat for Leghorn and Cadiz respectively, but with orders to call in at Lisbon to see if it was in their interest to sell their cargoes there: the Lisbon agent however directed them to continue their voyages 'a large fleet of Corn Ships having entirely dampt that Market'.[5] This practice was facilitated by the English treaty right of *franquia* which permitted vessels to lie in

[1] T. de T., M. dos N.E., Maço 6, Nos. 45-8. Ladings ceased in February 1766 on the prohibition of exports.

[2] Thomas Farrer and James Rondeau were both listed as 'Corn Factor' in *Kent's Directory* of 1765, and John Thompson as a 'Hop Factor'.

[3] For purposes of analysis the grain exporter is here regarded as different from the textiles trader although in practice many merchants fulfilled both functions.

[4] See Lisbon Factory memorials, 29 November 1764, P.R.O. C.O. 388/53, Ll. 24, 24 July 1765, C.O. 388/95, I.2.

[5] Undated memorial attached to Halifax to Hay, 11 May 1764, P.R.O. S.P. 89/59.

Portuguese harbours and store their grain or other commodities ashore for up to three months without payment of import duties.[1] It seems too that the merchant who was chiefly a grain exporter found it necessary to diversify his business much more than the cloth exporter, both in geographical and functional terms. Whereas the scale and stability of Portugal's demand for textiles could enable a merchant such as William Braund to concentrate his business to a high degree on its supply alone, the decidedly irregular nature and smaller scale of its grain needs forced the corn exporter to maintain contacts with a number of potential markets overseas, and to broaden his activities to be prepared for the years when English corn exports were at a low level or embargoed.

On arrival in Portugal the grain was sold to local wholesalers or retailers. Sales were made while cargoes were still on board ship as well as from warehouses.[2] Unlike English textiles, imports found essentially local markets. Some grain, however, was transhipped to Brazil: in 1753 it was noted that the 'Portuguese millers . . . buy up large Quantities of foreign Corn to turn into Flower . . . to be sent to the Brazils'.[3] Supplies were also required each year for provisioning the Portuguese mercantile fleets. In their sales for the metropolitan market the credit extended to purchasers was generally short, of no more than a few months. In the 1760s Holdsworth, Olive and Newman of Oporto disposed of most of their consignments from England at terms ranging from one or two months, to half-payments in two and four, or three and six months,[4] and in early September 1764 Charles Dodd of Lisbon sold a quantity of barley and Indian corn (the latter probably from North America) to Luiz Bartholomeu de Faria, one-half to be paid for the same month and the other by the end of the

[1] The value of this privilege is demonstrated by the strong feeling aroused among English merchants in such years as 1762-5 when the Portuguese government, in attempting to increase corn supplies, suspended it. Lisbon Factory memorial, 24 July 1765, P.R.O. C.O. 388/95, I.2.

[2] In 1753, during a time of feared dearth in Portugal and much governmental intervention in the Lisbon trade, the English Consul there wrote 'no Portuguese dare come to the [English merchants'] Warehouses to buy up large Quantities as They used to do . . . much less do they offer to purchase whole Cargoes at once whilst the Corn remains still on Ship-board'. Castres to Amyand, 6 October 1753, P.R.O. S.P. 89/48.

[3] Castres to Amyand, 22 September 1753, P.R.O. S.P. 89/48.

[4] H.R. (V.N.). Invoice and Sale Book, 1755-60, Current Account and Sales Book, 1764-9.

year.[1] Payments by the Portuguese were almost invariably made in cash or local commercial paper.

The English factors also engaged in the retail trade. This was recognized in the commercial treaties between the two countries, and appears to have been common, providing as it did an additional profit and a direct, if slow, method of selling off stocks. In 1701 an English visitor to Lisbon referring to the English merchants there noted 'their Corn they give out to ye market women and receive their int[erest?] every Saturday night'.[2] In 1715 the Oporto merchants complained that employees in their retail business were being wrongly molested by officials of the city's chamber of commerce;[3] and in August 1759 Gregory Olive of London was advised by Holdsworth, Olive and Newman of Oporto that they rather expected a consignment of his of rye to be a 'tedious Act^t', since rye had 'very little Expence' and they would be obliged to retail it.[1] It is not likely, however, that such dealings accounted for more than a small proportion of imports. The net proceeds of consignments were remitted to the exporting merchants, principally in bills of exchange or bullion; grain exporters in England and wine importers there broadly fell into two groups, with some exceptions in provincial ports where general merchanting was more common, so that returns in kind remained limited.

The English houses in Portugal also acted as grain importers, employing London and provincial firms as factors. Such business may have been substantial throughout the period as a consequence of its low capital needs and fairly rapid turnover. But probably more important were the joint ventures arranged by grain exporters in England and houses in Portugal. This business was attractive to both parties since it spread risks, and from the point of view of the English exporter, fostered greater diligence in Portugal. In 1759 and in the 1760s Holdsworth, Olive and Newman of Oporto engaged in several ventures of this kind, mainly with their principal grain consignor, William Parsons of Portsmouth.[5] Sometimes the initiative in such

[1] T. de T., F.F., Conserv. Ingles, Maço VI, Dodd *v.* Faria, f. 4.

[2] B.M. Add. MSS. 23,726, f. 22.

[3] Oporto Factory memorial, 18 May 1715, P.R.O. C.O. 388/20, P. 97.

[4] H.R. (V.N.). Letter Book, Dec. 1758-Oct. 1760. Letter of 25 August 1759. On this question, see also Lisbon Merchants' memorial, 12 April 1769, attached to Lyttelton to Weymouth, 6 May 1769, P.R.O. S.P. 89/68.

[5] H.R. (V.N.). Invoice and Sale Book, 1755-60; Current Account and Sale Book, 1764-9.

business came from the Oporto house. In October 1759, for example, Parsons was advised that prices were rising and that if he considered 'these Prices will answer', they were prepared, with another house in Oporto, to take a quarter-share in a cargo of 800-1,000 sacks of wheat, 50 barrels of flour and 100 sacks of bread.[1] On the dispatch of consignments Parsons drew bills of exchange on the Oporto firm for their share of the first cost, generally one-quarter or one-half, and in due course received his share of the net proceeds. Then too the more substantial Portuguese corn dealers also imported from England on their own account. In the early 1760s Holdsworth, Olive and Newman passed on orders from a number of Oporto dealers to their agent in London, including one for 100 bags of wheat for Carlos Puxotto in May 1761, and another for 100 bags each of wheat and rye for Antonio da Silva in December 1761.[2] For a small commission the agent saw to the shipments, drawing bills on the importer for their cost. It is likely that the proportion of grain shipments financed by English houses in Portugal and by Portuguese merchants increased after 1755, as happened in the textiles trade, and for the same reasons.

In the North American grain trade to Portugal the relative contribution of the mainland colonies at the end of the period can be seen in figures of shipping entering Lisbon in 1773.[3] Pennsylvania clearly led: altogether 44 ships came from Philadelphia, with ladings of 'Corn, Rice [and] Flour'. Then came Virginia with 16 ships with similar cargoes, Carolina with 14, laden with 'mostly Rice', and Maryland with 11 with varied grain cargoes including Indian corn. Quebec and New York were least important, sending only 6 and 4 ships, respectively, laden with corn.

It is likely that this trade was mainly financed by colonial merchants. English houses in Portugal were clearly preferred as factors, the employment of Portuguese firms being rare.[4] Among the English factors in Lisbon in 1768 were Parr and Bulkeley who acted for Henry Balle and Sons of James River, Virginia, and Moylan and Forrest who

[1] Ibid. Letter of 12 October 1759, Letter Book, Dec. 1758-Oct. 1760. See similar letters to Parsons of 29 March 1759, ibid., and 24 January 1761, Letter Book, Oct. 1760-Nov. 1765.

[2] Ibid. Letters to Gregory Olive of 7 May and 16 December 1761.

[3] Walpole to Rochford, 4 July 1774, Enclosure N.2, P.R.O. S.P. 89/77.

[4] In 1775 'not two Portuguese firms' served as factors for American firms, according to the Lisbon Envoy. Walpole to Rochford, 29 March 1775, P.R.O. S.P. 89/79.

were employed by consignors in Philadelphia and Maryland.[1] In Oporto in the 1760s Holdsworth, Olive and Newman were agents for several merchants including Amesbury and Bard of Halifax, Bayton, Wharton and Morgan of Philadelphia, and a number in Charleston where their connections were perhaps strongest.[2] Colonial consignments were disposed of in a similar way to those from England. Carolina rice sold by Holdsworth, Olive and Newman was usually paid for in half-payments at two and four months,[3] while on 10 March 1768 Parr and Bulkeley of Lisbon sold part of a wheat cargo from James River while it was still on board the vessel which had brought it 'for which the Money was receiv'd on the 2^{d} May', the remainder being sold in retail shops and in the corn market.[4] Some importing from North America was done by English firms in Lisbon and Oporto wholly on their own account,[5] while masters of ships engaged in the trade might also do a little business themselves; in April 1764, for example, ninety-seven barrels of the rice carried from Carolina to Oporto in Moses Pitt's command were on his account.[6] But, as would be expected, joint ventures between American merchants and factors in Portugal were common. In the 1760s Holdsworth, Olive and Newman frequently took one-third or one-half interests in rice cargoes from Charleston, although apparently their main aim in this was to expand their commission business.[7] The Oporto firm also imported Indian corn from Baltimore and Virginia on joint account with their London agents.[8] Joint ventures were also arranged between Charleston merchants and their London agents, as in one of August 1762 involving Smith, Brewton and Smith in

1 Voucher 9, Lisbon Factory memorial, 12 April 1769, P.R.O. S.P. 89/68.

2 They included Austin, Laurens and Appleby; Ward and Leger; Ancrum, Lance and Leacock; and Dawson and Dudley, to name but a few.

3 H.R. (V.N.). Current Account and Sale Book, 1764-9.

4 Voucher 9, Lisbon Factory memorial, 12 April 1769, P.R.O. S.P. 89/68.

5 In March 1769, for instance, Parr and Bulkeley of Lisbon imported a quantity of wheat and flour from Maryland. H.R. (V.N.). Account and Sale Book, 1769.

6 Ibid. Current Account and Sale Book, 1762-4.

7 In July 1764 the firm wrote to their London agent giving him 'full Power to agree wth Mr. Greenwood or any other good Houses in Carolina to take $\frac{1}{3}$ part of 1 or 2 Cargoes next year on our Acc^{t} . . . by taking $\frac{1}{3}$ we shall have the other $\frac{2}{3}$ds to our consignm^{t} & as our chief Motive for being concern'd in Rice is in ord^{r} to get Com[missio]^{ns} we would have it from diff^{t} Houses & from those that ship largely to this Place as it would be the means of getting the consig^{nmts} of the rest'. Ibid. Letter to G. Olive, 3 July 1764, Letter Book, Oct. 1760-Nov. 1765.

8 Ibid. Account and Sale Book, 1769-71.

Carolina and Smith and Nutt in London.[1] Triangular methods of financing the Carolina rice trade to Portugal were also practised. In 1765-6, for instance, the costs of consigning two cargoes of rice from Charleston to Oporto were shared one-third each between a merchant in Carolina, his agent in London and the Oporto factor.[2]

In part the colonial merchants received the proceeds of their shipments to Portugal in return shipments of Portuguese products, principally salt and wines. Returns to the colonies were also made in Portuguese coin.[3] However, the small extent of commodity shipments, the risk in remitting coin, and the difficulty in obtaining bills of exchange in Portugal payable in the colonies, indicate that the bulk of North American receipts were remitted to merchants' agents in England. About 1720 it was noted that the Philadelphia merchants generally had their returns for wheat and other products consigned to Lisbon 'by way of London or Bristol',[4] while Mathew Decker in the early 1740s observed that 'great part of the Payments' for American colonial corn shipments to Portugal 'centers in London'.[5] And Holdsworth, Olive and Newman's records contain numerous references to the practice: in 1760, for instance, remittances for three Carolina merchants for rice consignments were to be made to English agents,[6] and in 1762 the net proceeds of a rice shipment jointly financed by a Charleston merchant and his London agent were transferred to London.[7]

The other branch of the foodstuffs trade to Portugal was that in cod from Newfoundland and New England. In this period the English fishery at Newfoundland, and the associated commerce with southern Europe, continued to be dominated by merchants in England

[1] Ibid. Current Account and Sale Book, 1762-4.

[2] Respectively Brewton and Smith, John Nutt, and Holdsworth, Olive and Newman. Ibid. Current Account and Sale Book, 1764-9.

[3] In 1720 the Lieutenant-Governor of Maryland wrote that local merchants in their corn trade to Lisbon had 'their returns in money'. *Cal. S.P. Col. (A.W.I.)*, 1720-1, p. 130.

[4] Ibid., p. 210.

[5] *An Essay on the Causes of the Decline of the Foreign Trade*, p. 89.

[6] H.R. (V.N.). Letters to Austin, Laurens and Appleby, W. Lloyd, and Ogilvie and Forbes, 7 May 1760, Letter Book, Dec. 1758-Oct. 1760.

[7] Ibid. Current Account and Sale Book, 1762-4. The other reason for remitting via England is that indicated by Joshua Gee who in 1717 noted that the inhabitants of Philadelphia had 'of late' shipped large quantities of corn for Portugal and other parts of Europe 'to put themselves in a capacity of purchasing in England cloathing and other necessaries which they want'. *Cal. S.P. Col. (A.W.I.)*, 1716-17, p. 271.

particularly in the West Country. In the first half of the century a number of western ports were substantially involved in the trade, but after 1750 Poole and Dartmouth outstripped all others, becoming the two chief centres in England.[1] Dr Mathews has shown that until the century's last decades the West Country merchants in the main undertook the organization and finance of both the fishing and marketing operations. They paid for the fitting-out of the ships which sailed to Newfoundland early each spring, providing the necessary supplies and equipment and hiring the labour required locally. During the actual fishing season, which lasted from May to November, they often personally supervised the various activities centred on the island: the fishing conducted off its shores and on the Grand Bank, the curing of the catches, and the consignment of cargoes to markets in Portugal, Spain and Italy. On the return of the vessels to England, generally by the year's end, they began organizing the expedition for the coming season. The very considerable long-term capital investment essential to such enterprise – returns for consignments were not usually made until a year or more after the expeditions were fitted out – meant that the merchants involved generally specialized to a high degree in this business alone.[2]

As in the grain trade from England the masters of vessels carrying cod to Europe often received only the most general of instructions concerning their destination. In 1707 it was stated in Lisbon that the ships from Newfoundland and New England which put into Portuguese ports were often 'not bound to any certain Port, but [were] seeking for the best Market'.[3] The owners' instructions to the master of the *Guardian* galley which put into Oporto in October 1714 had been to go to 'Cadiz, up the Streights, or to such Place or Places he

[1] For a general discussion see H. A. Innis, *The Cod Fisheries* (New Haven, 1940), Chapters V-VII. I am indebted to Dr E. F. J. Mathews for permission to consult and draw on his unpublished University of London Ph.D. thesis (1957) on the 'Economic History of Poole, 1750-1850', Chapters IV and V.

[2] Concurrent with this traditional form of organization was the rise from the late seventeenth century of a system involving the growing body of fishermen settled permanently on the island, who helped man 'bye-boats' which fished for the cod which was then sold to the owners or hirers of 'sac' ships which carried the fish to market. On this development see, W. B. Stephens, *Seventeenth-Century Exeter* (Exeter, 1958), pp. 125-9.

[3] Lisbon Factory memorial, undated but written sometime in 1707, P.R.O. S.P. 89/89.

may find most to their advantage',[1] while in 1718 the commander of the *Neptune*, a Bideford ship, was ordered to proceed to 'Spain or Portugal' for a market.[2] Lisbon again was a common port of call.[3]

Undoubtedly Lisbon was the most important Portuguese market, followed by Oporto. The English consular survey of trade for 1772-3 put Lisbon's yearly imports of *bacalhau* at an average of 64,260 quintals valued at £30,100, while Oporto's averaged 44,400 quintals worth £26,640. Viana's imports in 1773 came to 16,900 quintals, while in the same year eleven ships unloaded *bacalhau* worth £6,800 at Figueira, and three ships discharged cargoes worth £1,200 at Aveiro. Caminha's imports in 1772-3 averaged £900.[4]

The remarkably full extant records for the 1750s and 1760s of the firm of Holdsworth, Olive and Newman of Oporto,[5] one of whose main lines of business was arranging the sale of Newfoundland cod consigned by West of England merchants, enable some detailed discussion of the second most important Portuguese market for cod. In the three seasons 1767-8, 1768-9 and 1769-70, 74 vessels in all unloaded cod in Oporto, nearly all from Newfoundland.[6] Of these 5 had home ports in America and the rest in England, chiefly the West of England. Dartmouth and Poole were pre-eminent with 21 and 17 vessels respectively, followed by Exeter/Topsham with 11, Teignmouth with 8, Weymouth 2 and Bristol 1. London and Liverpool led the other ports, each with 3 vessels.[7] In these seasons eight English firms in Oporto handled the trade, with Holdsworth, Olive and Newman the most important, dealing with some 60 per cent of the total landings of 136,800 quintals.[8] The firm's chief consignors

[1] Oporto Factory memorial, undated but received by the Board of Trade 9 July 1715, P.R.O. C.O. 388/20, P. 71.

[2] Memorial of R. Score, 17 September 1730, P.R.O. C.O. 388/90, A.42.

[3] '. . . all the Ships from Newfoundland and New England call in here for intelligence'. Letter of the Consul in Lisbon, Edward Hay, to Fox, 14 January 1756, P.R.O. S.P. 89/50.

[4] An Account of . . . all Goods imported into . . . Portugal from Great Britain and her Colonies, for 1772 and 1773. P.R.O. B.T. 6/62. In 1777 Lisbon's *bacalhau* imports came to 59,700 quintals, Oporto's to 47,700 quintals, Viana's to 11,900 and Figueira's to 6,500. *Arte e Diccionario do Commercio e Economia Portugueza*, p. 57.

[5] Kept in the Vila Nova offices of Hunt, Roope and Company, Oporto. Before 1761 the firm was known as Holdsworth and Olive, but for convenience has been referred to throughout in its later form.

[6] H.R. (V.N.). Rough Book, 1766-9. The lists used appear reliable, although it is possible they are not perfectly complete. A season ran from autumn to spring.

[7] For the full list, see Appendix VIII.

[8] See Appendix IX.

included members of the partners' families at Dartmouth: in the years 1755-60 the leading consignor among the forty doing business with the house was a Thomas Holdsworth, with thirteen shipments totalling 18,800 quintals, some 30 per cent of the house's business, and in 1767-70 the leading consignor was an Arthur Holdsworth followed by a Robert Newman. Despite these connections it is clear that the firm was independent of the Dartmouth merchants, and not an enterprise financed and controlled by them.[1] Other prominent Devon shippers were John Teage of Dartmouth and William and Gregory Jackson of Exeter, while the leading Poole shippers included Joseph and Samuel White and the firm of Clark and Young. The North American consignors included William Meany of Halifax, and Samuel Gray and Blanchard and Hancock of Boston. Throughout these years, in contrast to the other foodstuffs trades, the firm had virtually no direct financial interest in cod importing, but concentrated on its agency business.[2]

Holdsworth, Olive and Newman's dominating position in the Oporto cod trade led it to attempt to support prices by regulating the supply offered to buyers. In January 1765, for example, it wrote to one consignor that it had handled two-thirds of the 30,000 quintals received so far that season which 'has enabled us to support the prices from 3,400 *reis* to 3,650 *reis* [18s. 9d. to 19s. 9d.] p^r Quintal aboard'.[3] Nevertheless during a season prices could vary much owing to fluctuations in supply. Sometimes a period of weeks in which few or no ships arrived was followed by the simultaneous arrival of many, as at the beginning of October 1765 when the arrival of thirteen vessels 'quite glutted' the market and according to the firm so 'frighted our buyers that they'll not buy'.[4]

[1] The importance of family connections can be seen too in the appointment of John Olive's brother, Gregory Olive, as the firm's London agent between 1759 and 1770. One of his functions was to maintain and extend the business with merchants. On 30 June 1760 the Oporto house asked if he could 'spare a few days to take a trip down to Poole & speak to ye several Gent [lemen listed] acquaint them . . . of the present state of our market for fish & assure them of our readiness to serve them in w^t consignm^ts they shall please to favour us w^th'. H.R. (V.N.). Letter Book, Dec. 1758-Oct. 1760.

[2] In fact, a little surprisingly, joint ventures in the Newfoundland cod trade do not seem to have occurred to any degree.

[3] Ibid. Letter to W. Spurrier, 19 January 1765, Letter Book, Oct. 1760-Nov. 1765. See also letter to Clark & Young, 5 July 1759, Letter Book, Dec. 1758-Oct. 1760.

[4] Ibid. Letters to W. Spurrier and G. Jackson, 5 October 1765, Letter Book, Oct. 1760-Nov. 1765.

As well as sales to dealers in local markets, imported cod was sold to men supplying Portuguese vessels or exporting to Brazil. In March 1764 it was thought the coming season's fish 'will sell well as [there are] 25 Sail fitting out for ye Rio, Bahia and Pernambuco',[1] and in the following season it was hoped that such demands would reach 5-6,000 quintals.[2] The house also retailed cod, although in a small way only.[3]

Credit arrangements with the Portuguese cod dealers rarely extended beyond eight months, the most common terms being one-quarter or one-third of the total amount immediately in cash, with the balance at two, four and six months, or three and six months. Remittances were made to consignors in England in bills of exchange drawn on the firm's London agent, the bills being drawn at differing lengths of time from sight according to the terms of the agreement with the Portuguese buyer. The London agent was kept in funds by bills drawn on wine importers in England, either by the house itself or by other Oporto wine shippers who sold bills to the Oporto house. Remittances in bullion were confined to one or two leading consignors. Deductions from the amounts remitted to England were made, where applicable, for freight charges from Newfoundland paid by the firm, and for the unloading charges, consular levies and other local costs met by the house, together with its commission of 3 per cent. Merchants were often debited too for the cost of a lading of salt and a cask or two of wine and some fruit, but very few indeed of the English cod shippers imported wine as a business. A feature of the cod business at Oporto was the dilatoriness of the Portuguese in paying their debts. In January 1759 the firm wrote to a Poole merchant that they had sold a consignment of cod of his for one-third ready money and the remainder in three and six months. They added, however, that they would be 'very glad to get it in 8 m^ths^, the People of this Place never make any Acc^t^ of 2 or 3 months & really some do

[1] Ibid. Letter to A. Holdsworth, 31 March 1764.

[2] Ibid. Letter to C. Hake, 12 October 1765.

[3] The retailing of imported fish by English firms in Portugal was common. In Lisbon in 1701 it was noted that 'when the Merch^ts^ have Herrings or fish from Newfoundl^d^ cons^d^ y^m^ they retail it out in little lodges near ye waterside where they hire a man to attend it'. B.M. Add. MSS. 23,726, ff. 21-2. See also Oporto Merchants' memorial, 18 May 1715, P.R.O. C.O. 388/20, P. 97, and Lisbon Merchants' memorial, 12 April 1769, attached to Lyttelton to Weymouth, 6 May 1769, P.R.O. S.P. 89/68.

not of 6 or 8 mths or even 12 after agreement'.[1] Where the Oporto house itself ran the risk of dilatory payments or bad debts it charged an additional 2 per cent commission. Concerning the American cod consignors sometimes remittances of their balances were made in kind, but for the most part their balances were transferred to agents in England. In 1767, for example, the proceeds of consignments from Samuel Gray and Blanchard and Hancock of Boston were transferred to Watson and Olive of London and Devonshire and Reeve of Bristol respectively.[2]

While the organization, then, of the foodstuffs trades had much in common with the textile trade, there were some notable differences, in particular in terms of the ports engaged in the England-Portugal trade, and in the more flexible conduct of business by the merchants and factors involved.

[1] H.R. (V.N.). Letter to J. White, 6 January 1759, Letter Book, Dec. 1758-Oct. 1760. They further added that they could do better business if the terms of sale ran to nine months, and wished that 'all the Gentlemen that trade to Newfld [could] stay so long out of their money . . . but you know there are few that if not have their money soon they can't fit another Year, & to please them we give bills at 3 & 6 mths & some part ready money'.

[2] Ibid. Rough Book, 1766-9. Remitting to England was general in the colonial-American cod trade. In 1720 the proceeds of the Massachusetts merchants were 'remitted chiefly to Great Britain either pr bills of exchange or gold'. *Cal. S.P. Col.* (*A.W.I.*) 1719-20, p. 360, and in 1721 New Hampshire's receipts were 'generally remitted to [England] except what is returned in salt for the fishery'. Ibid., 1720-1, p. 411. And in the early 1760s 'bills of exchange [were] generally remitted to London for the proceeds of [the northern colonies'] best fish, sold in the Roman-catholic countries of Europe'. D. MacPherson, *Annals of Commerce*, Vol. III, p. 397.

5 *The Wine Trade*

THE BUSINESS PROBLEMS in the Portuguese wine trade to England differed quite markedly from those in the export trades from England. First, given the luxury nature of the product, once the trade with England had been established the market in England for Portuguese wines remained strictly limited. Then, since wines were far less homogeneous products than textiles or foodstuffs – marked variations in quality could occur not only from vintage to vintage but in the production of adjacent vineyards in the same vintage – there was a heightened need of expertise. This was accentuated by the ease with which wines lent themselves to adulteration and fraudulent dealing. Of much significance, too, was the heavy capital investment the trade required. This arose in part because of the change over the period away from the consumption of 'young' wines towards older, matured wines; and in part because of the high English import duties which amounted to roughly double the shipping prices from Portugal. These features made for a commercial organization, in which instead of there being, as in the textiles and, to a lesser extent, the foodstuffs trades, one dominant group of businessmen – the exporters in England – there existed two financially committed groups, shippers in Portugal and importers in England.

From the inception of the trade about 1690 Oporto was the premier exporting centre in Portugal.[1] By 1701 its yearly exports to London were put at about 14,000 pipes compared to some 6,000 pipes from Lisbon.[2] In the early years some of Oporto's exports were produced

[1] See memorial of the Portugal merchants of London, received by the Commissioners for Trade, 9 August 1692, P.R.O. C.O. 388/2, ff. 66-7. The volume and rapid growth of Oporto's total wine shipments from 1689 support this view. See J. Warre, *The Past, Present and Future State of the Wine Trade*, Appendix M.

[2] B.M. Add. MSS. 23,726, f. 18. The size of these figures suggests they include shipments to the English outports.

locally and in the Minho region, but the subsequent growth of the trade seems to have been based almost entirely on the development of the vineyards of the upper Douro region. By 1729 annual shipments from Oporto were estimated at 25,000 pipes worth £343,750 and from Lisbon, 5,000 pipes worth £60,500. Exports from Figueira were put at 1,500 pipes, valued at £18,560.[1] In the early 1750s Oporto and the Douro underwent a decline caused by intense competition from the other producing regions and disputes between the English shippers and the vineyard proprietors, but their pre-eminence was soon restored.[2] In 1772-3, shipments from Oporto averaged 20,030 pipes annually compared with 5,800 pipes from Lisbon.[3]

On the other hand, the position of the English importing centres was transformed during the period. In the early years London was outstanding: between 1698 and 1702 it handled over 88 per cent (by volume) of all Portuguese wines imported.[4] At this time London wine merchants, as well as meeting the demands of the capital, carried on a large intermediary business with provincial merchants.[5] However, as the demand for Portuguese wines became established so provincial merchants increasingly developed direct connections with Portugal and imported through local ports. This development was encouraged by the savings made in transport costs for this bulky product, and by a feature of the Customs system by which Portuguese wines brought into the outports paid lower duties than at London, to the extent of £3 9s. per tun[6] from 1697 to 1704 and £4 16s. thereafter. This difference in duties also undoubtedly encouraged London importers to land wines at other ports and bring them on to London. By 1738-42 imports into the combined outports had risen to an average of 4,900 tuns annually, compared to 790 tuns in 1698-1702, and London's share had fallen to 58 per cent. London's imports were

1 Attachment to Tyrawly to Newcastle, 26 June 1729, P.R.O. S.P. 89/35; B.N. Col. Pomb., Cod. 638, f. 461. These figures refer to exports to all the English possessions, amongst which the English market clearly predominated. Oporto's share of total wine shipments to England has been calculated as 67 per cent between 1704-12, and 76 per cent between 1737-44. J. de Macedo, *A Situação Económica no Tempo de Pombal*, p. 75.

2 For these developments, see ibid., p. 73 et seq., and V. M. Shillington and A. B. W. Chapman, op. cit., Part II, Chap. VI, *passim*.

3 Whitehead to Rochford, 30 April 1774, P.R.O. S.P. 89/76; Lisbon Factory account, 6 May 1774, P.R.O. B.T. 6/62. These figures also refer to all English territories.

4 This figure and those following are derived from P.R.O. Customs 3.

5 See T. S. Willan, *The English Coasting Trade, 1600-1750* (Manchester, 1938), p. 106.

6 A tun was equivalent to two pipes.

1. Lisbon in 1752

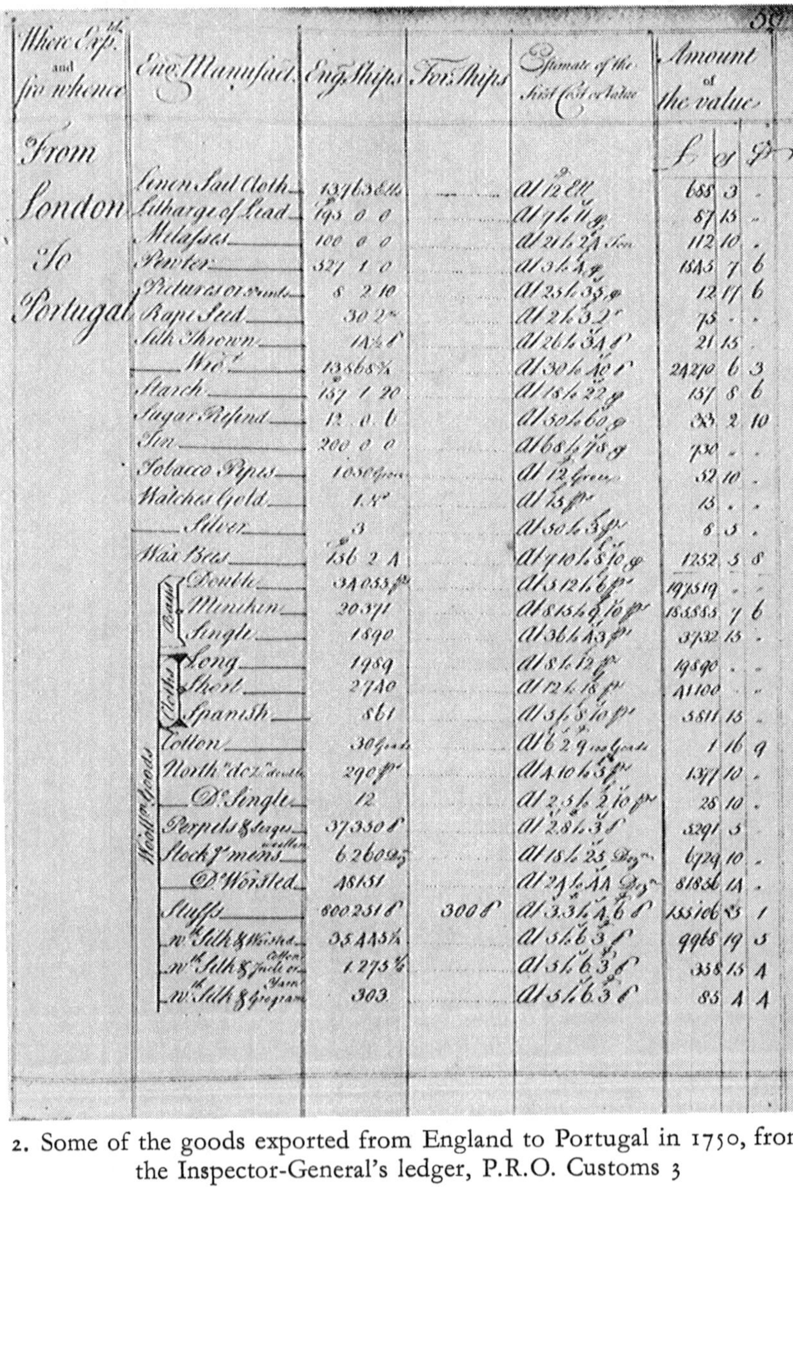

Where Exp.th and fro whence	Eng. Manufact.	Eng. Ships	For. Ships	Estimate of the first Cost or Value	Amount of the value £	s	d
From London To Portugal							
	Linen Sail Cloth	13763 Ells	—	At 12d Ell	688	3	-
	Litharge of Lead	195 0 0		At 7s & 11s	87	15	-
	Melasses	100 0 0		At 21s & 24s Ton	112	10	-
	Pewter	327 1 0		At 3l [illegible]	1845	7	6
	Pictures or Prints	8 2 10		At 25s & 35s	12	17	6
	Rape Seed	30 Qrs		At 2l & 3l	75	-	-
	Silk Thrown	14½ lb		At 26s & 34s lb	21	15	-
	Wrot	13868¾		At 30s & 40s lb	24270	6	3
	Starch	157 1 20		At 18s & 22s	157	8	6
	Sugar Refind	12 0 6		At 50s & 60s	33	2	10
	Tin	200 0 0		At 68s & 78s	730	-	-
	Tobacco Pipes	1050 Gross		At 12d Gross	52	10	-
	Watches Gold	1 Nº		At 15l pr	15	-	-
	Silver	3		At 50s & 3l pr	8	5	-
	Wax Bees	136 2 4		At 7l 10s & 8l 10s	1252	5	8
	Woollen Goods: Bays Double	34055 pcs		At 5l 12s & 6l pr	197519	-	-
	Minikin	20371		At 8l 15s & 9l 10s pr	155555	7	6
	Single	1890		At 36s & 43s pr	3732	15	-
	Cloths Long	1989		At 8l & 12l pr	19890	-	-
	Short	2740		At 12l & 18l pr	41100	-	-
	Spanish	861		At 5l & 8l 10s pr	5811	15	-
	Cotton	30 yards		At 6d 2s 9d [illegible] yards	1	16	9
	Northern dozens double	290 pcs		At 4l 10s & 5l pr	1377	10	-
	Do Single	12		At 2l 5s & 2l 10s pr	25	10	-
	Perpets & Serges	37330 lb		At 2s 8d & 3s lb	5291	5	
	Stockings mens woollen	6260 9/12		At 18s & 25s Dozn	6729	10	-
	Do Worsted	48151		At 24s & 44s Dozn	81856	18	-
	Stuffs	600251 lb	300 lb	At 3s 3d & 4s 6d lb	155106	3	1
	wth Silk & Worsted	35445½		At 5s & 6s 3d lb	9968	19	5
	wth Silk & Cotton Inkle or Yarn	1275½		At 5s & 6s 3d lb	358	15	4
	wth Silk & Grogram	303		At 5s & 6s 3d lb	85	4	4

2. Some of the goods exported from England to Portugal in 1750, from the Inspector-General's ledger, P.R.O. Customs 3

3. Lord Tyrawly in 1712

4. Oporto about 1750

5. Carriage of wine on the Douro, *c.* 1780

6. Contemporary model of an 80-gun English warship on the establishment of 1719

GOLD

(a) *Dobra*. 12,800 *reis*. Minas Gerais Mint
(b) *Moeda*. 4,000 *reis*
(c) Half *Moeda*. 2,000 *reis*. Rio de Janeiro Mint
(d) Quarter *Moeda*. 1,000 *reis*. Bahia Mint
(e) *Crusado Novo*. 400 *reis*

SILVER

(f) *Crusado*. 400 *reis*

7. Portuguese coins of the reign of Dom João V (1706-1750)

8. Falmouth packet-boat of the end of the eighteenth century

9. Cod fishing off North America about 1770

10. Arthur Holdsworth, merchant of Dartmouth (centre), with one of his captains (right), about 1760

exceeded for the first time by the outports in 1753, and this became an annual feature after 1765. By 1768-72, the capital's imports were declining absolutely and its share had contracted to 46 per cent.[1] Further light is thrown on the rise of the outports by an official table of imports into all English ports between 1711 and 1731.[2] In 1711-13 thirty-eight provincial ports imported directly from Portugal, the great majority handling only small quantities, and only four importing on average more than 100 tuns annually, namely Kings Lynn, Bristol, Exeter, and Hull, the former leading with 241 tuns.[3] By 1729-31, 44 ports were engaged and 10 imported more than 100 tuns annually. Southampton now led with 542 tuns, followed by Bristol with 538, Hull with 498, Kings Lynn with 475, Yarmouth with 331, and Exeter with 281.[4]

The great bulk of shipments to England throughout the period to 1770 were made to the order and account of English wine merchants in London and the provinces. Very little exporting was undertaken by the Portuguese on their own account because of their poor financial resources and their indifferent knowledge of the English market.[5] The scale of London's wine consumption and its distributive trade, coupled with the investment the business demanded and the need for close personal attention, meant that the London merchants

[1] London's imports then averaged 5,220 tuns annually, and the outports 6,250 tuns. In 1752 an Act was passed requiring that Portuguese and other wines landed at the outports and sent to within twenty miles of the Royal Exchange should pay the extra duty payable on wines imported into London. Although it should have lessened the transit trade from the outports to London, the Act may have been much evaded. In 1777 it was pointed out that 'the fraudulent Trader lands his wine at Rochester and other places near London, or even so far as Southampton and Scotland, and conveys it clandestinely thither by Land carriage and even Coastwise as Cyder or other Liquors, trusting to the Carelessness or Corruption of the Officers; so that this [extra] Duty is . . . almost entirely lost'. A further problem was the 'difficulties caused to Gentlemen and others not engaged in Trade, who, being unacquainted with the . . . Law, find their Wine seized when (as they thought) they were very innocently removing it from their Cellar in the Country to their House in Town'. B.M. Add. MSS. 8133B, f. 374.

[2] Chol. (H.). MSS., Cambridge. P. 28, 13/1-13/7.

[3] The others imported 174, 164 and 144 tuns respectively.

[4] The others were Chester – 174, Boston – 159, Dover – 153, and Liverpool – 115 tuns.

[5] In February 1756 the English Envoy in Lisbon considered the Portuguese were not concerned in any Mercantile Transaction in regard to their Wines. Hay to Fox, 11 February 1756, P.R.O. S.P. 89/50. But undoubtedly some exporting was done on their account. Between 1732 and 1735, for example, Francisco Pedroza of Oporto shipped some 270 pipes annually on average to an agent in London, Bento Demages. B.N. Col. Pomb., Cod. 625, ff. 7-28, 36-7. A further deterrent to Portuguese enterprise was that aliens importing wines into England had to pay an additional duty of £1. 12s. a tun.

often specialized in the wine trade as such or even in one of its branches. In 1694, for instance, of the one hundred wine merchants in the City some apparently specialized in either the Portuguese or the Spanish trade.[1] The medium-sized and smaller merchants, though, often engaged in other lines of business, and in the provinces wine importing was invariably combined with other business. The merchants placed their orders overwhelmingly with the English houses in Oporto, Lisbon and the other centres, who did business as wine shippers. Portuguese wine shippers seem to have been rare, for reasons similar to those discouraging them as exporters.[2] Few if any of the English firms concentrated on wine shipping alone, even in Oporto. One of the leading shippers there at the end of the 1770s, Offley, Campion and Brooks, for example, regularly did business as a factor in the textiles trade from England and occasionally handled consignments of corn and codfish.[3] Direct correspondence between shippers and importers was supplemented by the shippers' London agents. Sometimes these were partners in the Oporto or Lisbon firm; alternatively, they were independent firms working for a commission.

The wines shipped were selected from stocks held by the shippers before orders were received from England. This practice was due to the variability of the product and the possibilities of fraudulent dealing, which meant that before placing orders merchants wanted a clear indication of the quality and price of the wines available and preferably something to taste as well. The holding of stocks also assured shippers of a supply of the best or most marketable wines, and greater consistency in their shipments. A little of the wine came from the few vineyards owned by Englishmen in Portugal,[4] with the rest from Portuguese vineyard proprietors. In the upper Douro these ranged from a few great landowners, secular and ecclesiastical, whose estates yielded large quantities, to many small peasants producing a few pipes only. In the weeks following the vintage, normally held in

1 Reasons . . . why no further Duty or Excise be laid upon Wines. P.R.O. C.O. 388/3, E.29.

2 The weak Portuguese shipping position in Oporto was somewhat improved in 1756 with the setting-up of the Companhia Geral de Agricultura dos Vinhos do Alto Douro whose activities included shipping wines to England and Ireland. Between 1764 and 1768, however, its shipments averaged only 225 pipes annually. R.C.V.P. Livro dos Despachos da Alfandega de 1762, f. 41 et seq.

3 O.F. (V.N.). Journal and Waste Books, 1779-85.

4 For details of such ownership, see pp. 131-2.

late September or October, the English shippers or their Portuguese brokers customarily made a number of trips into the upper Douro where they inspected the newly-made wines and made their purchases. Until 1756 this business was little regulated, but thereafter the Companhia Geral de Agricultura dos Vinhos do Alto Douro restricted the purchase of wines for export to strictly demarcated areas.[1] Many transactions were often involved. For instance, one of the smallest shippers at the end of the period, Holdsworth, Olive and Newman, in their purchases of only 405 pipes of red and white wines of the 1770 vintage had dealings with some 15 suppliers,[2] while at the end of the 1770s, Offley, Campion and Brooks, whose purchases of the '78, '79, and '80 vintages ranged between 3,000 and 4,000 pipes, dealt with some 90, 100 and 120 suppliers respectively.[3]

In the early, expansive years of the trade the Douro and Minho growers enjoyed a strong bargaining position which turned payment terms in their favour. An English visitor to the region in 1704 noted that immediate payment for wines was then the rule,[4] and in 1715 the Oporto Factory in representing their urgent need for permission to carry such arms as they pleased when in the upper Douro 'amongst those barbarous Mountaineers', spoke of their obligation 'to travel with great Sums of Money for the purchasing of Wines'.[5] The planting of new vineyards, however, weakened the growers' position and led them to extend credit to the shippers. At the end of the 1730s John Hitchcock, an Oporto shipper, did not usually finally settle his wine debts until about Michaelmas,[6] and at the end of the 1760s Holdsworth, Olive and Newman customarily paid for their wines in one-third instalments, at 'Loading' (that is sometime in March or April when the pipes stored in the upper Douro until the winter floods were past could be safely loaded on boats for Oporto), at the feast of St John (24 June), and at Michaelmas.[7] Payments were normally made

[1] J. de Macedo, *A Situação Económica no Tempo de Pombal*, pp. 79 80; V. M. Shillington and A. B. W. Chapman, op. cit., pp. 268-9.

[2] H.R. (V.N.). Wine Purchase Book, 1768-74.

[3] O.F. (V.N.). Waste Book, 1779-85. Most of the transactions were quite small, the largest being for 252 pipes of '78 red wine bought of Alvaro Pinto of Sanhoana.

[4] Diary of Thomas Woodmass, quoted by C. Sellers, *Oporto, Old and New* (1899), p. 24.

[5] Oporto Factory memorial, 1 February 1715, P.R.O. C.O. 389/25, f. 127.

[6] P.R.O. C.M.E. C.110 19, 20, Pratt *ex parte*, Hitchcock to Hitchcock, 5 September 1739, 4 June 1740, 2 July 1740.

[7] H.R. (V.N.). Wine Purchase Book, 1768-74.

in cash, or by bills of exchange that the growers drew upon shippers.

From the beginning the shippers in Oporto needed sizeable capitals for their business. In the early decades of the period the Portuguese wines drunk in England were a year or less old.[1] Shippers therefore only held the stocks bought after each vintage for a few months before shipment.[2] In fixing shipping prices note was taken of the first cost of the wines, carriage and loading expenses, cooperage, and port charges and duties, and a commission was charged. Shippers usually settled their accounts with importers by drawing bills on them: the credit that was given varied, but from the beginning of the period full payment was generally required about six months after the wines were shipped. In 1739 a Northampton wine merchant complained of the short credit given by his Oporto shipper and referred to the practice of the 'Topp houses' at Lisbon who drew bills at six months usance,[3] and about the same time Tilden and Thompson of Oporto were drawing bills for one-third amounts of accounts at one month, three months and a year.[4] The bills were mostly drawn to the order of the shippers' London agents, who remitted the funds they received to Portugal. Thus, in the very early years of the trade when the growers obtained immediate payments for their wines, shippers did not receive payment from England until about a year later, and in the decades immediately following when the growers gave credit for some six months, the shippers were out of their capital also for about six months.

From about 1730 the capital needs of the Oporto shippers grew. This development was associated with the innovation of adding brandy to the Douro wines, which hastened their evolution from beverage into dessert wines which improved with age, and as such made them similar to present-day ports.[5] The consequent growth of

[1] A. L. Simon, *Bottlescrew Days* (1926), pp. 51, 55-7, 109-10.

[2] Dowker and Stuckey's shipments from Oporto in the years about 1710 to Robert Wilmot in London were invariably of the preceding vintage. O.F. (Lond.). R. Wilmot's Ledger. See also Oporto Merchants' memorial, received in London 9 July 1715, P.R.O. C.O. 388/20, P. 71, and Reasons . . . why no further Duty or Excise be laid upon Wines [1694], P.R.O. C.O. 388/3, E.29.

[3] P.R.O. C.M.E. C.110, 19, 20, Pratt *ex parte*, Pratt to Hitchcock, 9 December 1739.

[4] Ibid., Stanhope to Hitchcock, 31 March 1739. See also Hitchcock to Hitchcock, 14 November 1739.

[5] This innovation is normally and rather tentatively dated from about 1730, A. L. Simon, *Bottlescrew Days*, pp. 119-20, and some evidence has come to light to confirm

English demand for older wines was reflected in merchants' orders to shippers. During the later 1730s, for example, the great bulk of John Hitchcock's shipments from Oporto each year were still of the preceding vintage,[1] but by the later 1760s Holdsworth, Olive and Newman's were mostly two or three vintages old.[2] And in 1776 the Companhia Geral de Agricultura dos Vinhos do Alto Douro was offering English importers wines from any vintage between 1771 and 1775.[3] The competition among shippers for business made it necessary for them to hold stocks for much longer periods. A Portuguese survey of the Oporto shippers' business enables this to be shown for 1771.[4] At the end of December 1770 the shippers' stocks in Oporto totalled 19,980 pipes: since the produce of any vintage was not brought to the city until the following spring these wines were at least of the '69 vintage, i.e. already over a year old. In 1771 the survey records 22,090 pipes of the '70 vintage as brought to Oporto, while 19,138 pipes were exported to the 'North', leaving 23,321 pipes in stock.[5] Exports in 1771 thus roughly comprised the stock at the end of 1770. Since shipments now largely took place between spring and the year's end,[6] the wines shipped in 1771 were mostly over eighteen months old.[7]

this. In 1724 the English Consul at Lisbon wrote of the Oporto white wines as 'all mixt & strengthened with Brandys' but that this was not the case with the red wines. Burnett to Newcastle, 6 August 1724 N.S., P.R.O. S.P. 89/31. And in 1734 an English merchant complained of wines shipped from Oporto, almost certainly including red wines, which 'taste too much of brandy'. P.R.O. C.M.E. C.110, 19, 20, Pratt *ex parte*, Pratt to Hitchcock, 12 September 1734. In 1742 the Lisbon Consul lamented the 'wines . . . to be had at Oporto are mixed with Brandy to that degree as not to be drinkable . . . I have been obliged for my own use to take up with a few dozen of very indifferent claret, till we have a new vintage.' Castres to Stone, 1 July 1742 N.S., P.R.O. S.P. 89/42. The introduction about this time of the cylindrical bottle, which, unlike the traditional broad-bottomed, bulbous-shaped bottle, enabled wines to be laid down to mature, may also have assisted. A. L. Simon, op. cit., pp. 120, 236.

1 P.R.O. C.M.E. C.110, 19, 20, Pratt *ex parte*, *passim*.

2 H.R. (V.N.). Shipments Invoice Book, 1761-9.

3 A. L. Simon, op. cit., p. 141; Archer to Dottering, 24 June 1776, P.R.O. S.P. 89/83. See also J. Croft, *A Treatise on the Wines of Portugal* (York, 1788), p. 13.

4 B.N. Col. Pomb., Cod. 638, f. 133. Although the survey refers to '*commerciantes estrangeiros*' it seems clear that all the firms listed were English with possibly one or two exceptions.

5 These figures must be regarded with caution, since if the 1770 stock figure, and the purchase and export figures were correct, there should have been 22,932 pipes in stock at the end of 1771.

6 See Chapter 8, p. 110.

7 At the end of September 1764, Holdsworth, Olive and Newman's stock of wines totalled 175 pipes, the vintage year of 152 being given; of these 61 per cent were '63 wines, 28 per cent '62, 7 per cent '61, and 4 per cent '60. At the end of August 1771

At this time the credit extended to merchants in England probably remained unchanged at about six months: Holdsworth, Olive and Newman's practice in the early 1760s, for example, was to draw bills on importers for this period.[1] So that from the 1730s although the Oporto shippers were then receiving six months credit from the Portuguese vineyard proprietors they were not generally paid for their shipments until over two years later. Their capital was now tied up for over eighteen months at a time. In the 1770s it seems still older wines were being shipped – at the end of the decade over two and a half years' old on the average in the case of one shipper[2] – and the investment period could have lengthened to over two and a half years.

By the 1770s a large shipper in Oporto needed a large capital. Such information is available for Offley, Campion and Brooks, one of the leading shippers at the end of the decade. In 1779 and 1780 their shipments averaged 4,371 pipes annually, and in 1779 their proprietary capital was 241,809 *milreis*, some £66,500.[3] No other business they did tied up their capital to any extent so that this sum would have been almost entirely devoted to wine shipping. Some rough calculations bear this out. The price the firm paid for wines varied but was generally about 25 *milreis* or £7 a pipe. With wines held in Oporto for some two and a half years before shipment, and with shipments of over 4,000 pipes annually, a capital of £66,500 would have been barely sufficient.

Increasing capital needs probably mainly explain the notable degree of concentration in the shipping business at Oporto about 1770. In 1771[4] some forty-seven English firms were engaged in wine shipping, although only thirty-nine actually shipped abroad in that year. The four leading houses accounted for 40 per cent of the total shipments – they were Charles Etty with 2,582 pipes, Oliver Beckett with 2,053, John Clies with 1,673, and William Warre with 1,391. The leading eight firms shipped 58 per cent of the total, and the leading twelve, 70 per cent.

560 pipes were held: 68 per cent were of the '70 vintage, 22 per cent '69, 9 per cent '68 and 1 per cent '67. H.R. (V.N.). Rough Journal, 1761-6, f. 113, and Wine Book, 1771-7.

1 Ibid., Letter Book, Oct. 1760-Nov. 1765, *passim.*

2 O.F. (V.N.). Journal and Waste Books, 1779-85.

3 Ibid., Waste Book, 1779-85, f. 55.

4 B.N. Col. Pomb., Cod. 638, f. 133.

The merchants in England also needed considerable capitals to conduct their business. To start with there were the large payments attending the landing of their wines. These included the cost of carriage from Portugal: in peacetime the rate was usually about 30s. a tun, but in wartime it might be double or treble this figure.[1] Then there were the unloading and port charges. And finally, the import duties: on a tun of wine these amounted to roughly double the shipping prices from Portugal and on a big consignment could total many hundreds of pounds. Sometimes merchants sold the wines on the quayside, especially when demand was brisk. But usually it was carried to vaults where it was 'fined' and prepared for sale. In addition to private sales wines were sold at auction. One held 'by the Candle' in September 1713 at Lloyd's Coffee House included fifteen pipes of 'Excellent new Red Oporto Wines, deep, bright, strong, fresh and neat',[2] while another announced in the *Daily Advertiser* in early May 1741 offered thirteen pipes of 'extraordinary good red Oporto Wine of the Vintage 1739' which had just been landed.[3]

The merchants' business varied much according to its scale and location. The great London men were mainly wholesalers selling to other middlemen in the capital and provinces as well as to local vintners and taverners. The medium and smaller London men, and nearly all the provincial merchants, did both a wholesale and retail trade, supplying neighbouring vintners and taverners and often competing with one or both of them. The credit given by merchants no doubt varied, but the evidence points to six months as normal. Payments by vintners and others to Robert Wilmot between 1708 and 1714 varied between a few months to a year or more after purchase, but usually all or the greater part was made within about six months.[4] Since merchants generally received similar credit from their suppliers in Portugal additional capital needs to those already described depended on the time wines were stored before sale. In the early decades, as with the shippers, it seems likely they were held only a

[1] See Chapter 8, pp. 121-2, for a further discussion.

[2] C. Sellers, op. cit., p. 220.

[3] P.R.O. C.O. 388/40, Aa. 48.

[4] O.F. (Lond.). R. Wilmot's Ledger, *passim*. In the provinces wintry weather could cause payment to be postponed. In January 1740 a Leeds merchant wrote 'the badness of the weather has made the roads so very deep and full of water that was obliged to return . . . home again from collecting my debts in the country'. P.R.O. C.M.E. C.110 19, 20, Pratt *ex parte*. Hutchinson to Hitchcock, 3 January 1740.

short while. But as the taste for older wines developed so they were probably kept by merchants for increasing periods of time. Thus, it seems that the importers too became more capitalized over the period.

In contrast to their practice in the textiles and foodstuffs trades the English houses in Oporto did not deal in wines on their own account to any extent. Such enterprise was discouraged by the greater capital needed to export wine to England compared to importing English produce, especially since even a small shipper already needed substantial sums. Another factor was the serious problems involved in getting satisfactory service from agents in England, or in managing a shipping business in Portugal and simultaneously developing in England the personal relations and goodwill essential to a wholesale business in a restricted market. Wine importers too may well have discriminated against shippers who competed with them. The problem of capital supply probably discouraged also joint-account trading. Moreover, there is no evidence that wine merchants in England set up branches in Portugal in this period, although many merchants and shippers were familially connected. Some English importers may, however, have been financially interested in shipping firms. In 1779, for example, Richard Tydell, one of Offley, Campion and Brooks' principal customers in England, held a 3/13th share in the Oporto firm.[1] Thus it seems that the two groups in the wine trade, the shippers in Portugal and the merchant importers in England, very largely specialized on their respective business functions, as in fact they still do today.

[1] O.F. (V.N.). Waste Book, 1779-85, f. 61.

6 *The Employment of Merchant Shipping*

THE LARGE VOLUME of transactions in the textiles, foodstuffs and wine trades between England and Portugal necessitated the employment of a considerable volume of merchant shipping.[1] Over the period to 1770 some distinct changes occurred in the character of this shipping, in its total tonnage, in the size of the vessels involved, and in their nationality. Numerous vessels were also engaged in the North American trades with Portugal: this tonnage substantially contributed to the overall efficiency with which shipping was employed in Anglo-Portuguese trade.

There are no regular yearly figures available of the shipping movements in Anglo-Portuguese trade. But the scattered figures that are extant indicate, as can be seen in Table IV, that the vessels annually engaged in the trade between England and Portugal showed some decrease in number over the period, although, because of a resort to larger ships, the total tonnage employed became greater.

The differences between the two periods in the numbers of shipping involved were due in part to a higher level of grain exports in the later 1710s,[2] and a somewhat higher general level of transactions in the England-Portugal trade,[3] but their effect was limited. The disparity between the numbers of vessels clearing England for Portugal compared to those entering, apparent in both the later 1710s and the early 1770s, would have been typical of the period. It sprang from the

[1] Although bullion was shipped from Portugal to England in merchant vessels it was mainly carried in the Falmouth-Lisbon packet-boats and in warships. Discussion of these specialized shipping practices is found in Chapter 7.

[2] In 1715-17 English wheat exports to Portugal averaged 21,600 quarters annually compared to 1,800 quarters annually in 1771-5.

[3] See above, p. 16, Table II.

Table IV

CLEARANCES FROM ENGLISH PORTS FOR PORTUGAL, 1715-17 (ANNUAL AVERAGES)			CLEARANCES FROM BRITISH PORTS FOR PORTUGAL AND MADEIRA, 1771-5 (ANNUAL AVERAGES)		
Number	*Total Tonnage*	*Average Tonnage per Vessel*	*Number*	*Total Tonnage*	*Average Tonnage per Vessel*
230	17,160	75	161	18,873	117

ENTRIES INTO ENGLISH PORTS FROM PORTUGAL, 1718-19 (ANNUAL AVERAGES)			ENTRIES INTO BRITISH PORTS FROM PORTUGAL AND MADEIRA, 1771-5 (ANNUAL AVERAGES)		
Number	*Total Tonnage*	*Average Tonnage per Vessel*	*Number*	*Total Tonnage*	*Average Tonnage per Vessel*
312	19,995	64	291	27,908	96

Sources: P.R.O. C.O. 390/8B; C.O. 390/5, Part I, f. 71; B.T. 6/185. For the annual position in certain of these categories, see Appendixes X-XII. The vessels clearing for and entering from Madeira would have been fairly small in number.

employment in the inward trade to England of English and colonial-American vessels that had earlier arrived in Portugal from North America, and is discussed further below.

The relative importance of London and the outports, and the Portuguese ports, in terms of their shipping movements, can be shown for one or two years. In 1715-17 the vessels annually clearing from London and the outports for Portugal averaged 112 and 117 in number respectively: London's vessels were substantially larger at an average of 85 tons compared to the outports' 65 tons. The parity in clearances between London and the outports contrasts with the minor role of the outports in the textile trade from England, and is mainly explained by the provincial exports of grain and coal and the practice of sending ships only partly-laden to Portugal, their chief concern being to bring back wine. The outports from which vessels sailed for Portugal in these years can be shown: Exeter led with an annual average of 18 clearances, followed by Newcastle with 10, Bristol with 8, and Southampton and Kings Lynn with 7 each.[1]

[1] For the full list of outports, see Appendix XIII.

Of the clearances from English ports for Portugal in 1715-17, 99 vessels annually on the average were declared for Lisbon, 68 for Oporto, 9 for Figueira, 7 for Viana, 3 for Aveiro and 2 for Faro, the remaining 42 clearing for Portugal.[1] Oporto's position as the leading wine exporting centre is reflected in London's entries in 1717-19. Of the annual average of 180 ships, Oporto was the last port of call for 88 and Lisbon for 63, with the other ports far behind.[2]

In peacetime the vessels in the trade between England and Portugal were overwhelmingly of English ownership, although over the period there was a slight increase in the use of foreign vessels. Of the clearances from England in 1715-17 only one was foreign-owned, and one also of the entries into London from Portugal in 1717.[3] In 1771-5 of the clearances from British ports to Portugal and Madeira twelve vessels a year on the average were foreign, and seven of the entries.[4] During the major wars fought by England with France and Spain, however, the reduction in the supply of English merchant vessels brought about by the demands of the navy, the delays attending the convoy system, and enemy action, led to a marked resort to foreign shipping. The position during the Seven Years War, as reflected in Lisbon's total shipping movements, can be seen in Table V.

Table V ENGLISH VESSELS
ENTERING AND CLEARING LISBON, 1749-1770

	Number Entering (annual average)	*English Entries as Percentage of Total Entries*	*Number Clearing (annual average)*	*English Clearances as Percentage of Total Clearances*
1749-55	506	58	473	57
1756-63	319	37	303	38
1764-70	435	50	425	49

Source: Data drawn from J. de Macedo, 'Portugal e a Económia "Pombalina", Temas e Hipóteses', *Rev. de H.*, Vol. XIX (1954), Table 1.

The relative decline in the employment of English vessels during the war occurred despite the record levels of business attained. The dispatches of the English Consuls in Portugal bear out this picture.

1 For the annual figures, for London and the outports, see Appendix XIV.
2 For the annual figures, see Appendix XV.
3 P.R.O. C.O. 390/8B; C.O. 390/5, Part I, f. 71.
4 P.R.O. B.T. 6/185. For the annual figures, see Appendixes XI and XII.

In July 1756 the Consul in Oporto reported that 'the Portuguese encouraged by the long Delay of the Convoy are fitting out Ships with a design of having their Goods from England in their own Bottoms'.[1] And two years later, according to the Lisbon Consul, the trade from England was 'chiefly carried on in Neutral Ships' due to their ability 'when loaded immediately [to] proceed . . . without delays [while] British Ships for want of Convoys . . . are laying in our Harbour for Six or Eight Months'.[2] During the minor war between England and Spain in 1718-19, however, the normal predominance of English shipping was little affected.[3]

Throughout the years to 1770 numerous English and colonial-American vessels were employed each year in the cod and grain trades from North America to Portugal. Figures of the numbers involved are not available before the 1760s but in any one year they would not have been small. In the 1760s with the increase in grainstuff shipments from North America they would have grown. In 1765-8, in fact, 118 English and colonial-American ships on the average annually entered Lisbon from North America,[4] and in 1772-3, 151.[5] This tonnage contributed to the efficiency of employment of shipping in the trades between England and Portugal. In these trades a disparity often existed between the volume of shipping space that the outward trade from England required compared to the inward trade from Portugal. Despite their great value exports of English textiles did not need very much shipping space, and except when the amount was increased by a high level of grain exports, the space needed was less than that needed for the bulky Portuguese exports to England,

[1] Porrett to Fox, 10 July 1756, P.R.O. S.P. 89/50.

[2] Frankland to Pitt, 20 August 1758, P.R.O. S.P. 89/51. The dislocation of shipping in wartime and the resort to convoys is discussed in Chapter 8. In the midst of an earlier war with Spain, the English Consul in Lisbon, Abraham Castres, lamented that his income, depending as it did on the volume of English shipping as well as trade entering the Tagus, had been 'most wretched . . . our Navigation . . . is but low at present (though trade goes on as it used to do)'. He thought that in two or three years his Consulship might again prove 'flourishing' since in all likelihood the neutral ships then employed would be discarded, but 'if . . . we are to have a french war, which as a good Englishman I heartily wish for, the Consul must retire into the Country, and keep close till the storm be over'. Castres to Stone, 20 January 1744, P.R.O. S.P. 89/44.

[3] P.R.O. C.O. 390/5, Part I, ff. 72-5. Only 4 of the 220 annual clearances from English ports for Portugal were foreign-owned, and only 2 of the 312 entries.

[4] Lyttelton to Weymouth, 13 March 1769, Attachments 1-4, P.R.O. S.P. 89/67.

[5] Walpole to Rochford, 4 July 1774, Enclosures N. 1-2, P.R.O. S.P. 89/77. In these years on the average forty-five vessels annually came from Newfoundland.

wines in particular, but including also fruit, cork, shumack and salt. This disparity was accentuated by seasonal differences in commercial activity. Although the outward commerce from England was active throughout the year, it tended to be busiest in its second half, while exporting from Portugal was carried on fairly steadily through the year.[1]

The need, however, to send out numerous only partly-laden vessels from England to bring back wines was much reduced by the arrival in Portugal each year of the vessels from North America. The English-owned vessels were naturally interested in the possibility of freights to England and so apparently were many of the colonial-owned ships.[2] That substantial numbers of vessels were so employed in carrying cargoes to England can be seen in 1773, when 139 vessels entered Lisbon from North America and only 52 cleared the port for North America.[3] Supporting evidence for this practice is to be found in Holdsworth, Olive and Newman's records. Of the English and colonial-American vessels which came with consignments from North America for this Oporto house in the 1760s, some returned directly to America but most sailed to England, or to Dutch, German and other northern European ports, with ladings of wine and fruit.[4] Thus the tonnage in the North American-Portugal trades, as well as raising the efficiency of employment of shipping in the England-Portugal trade, also increased its own profitability by the cargoes it carried northwards from Portugal.

[1] See Chapter 8, pp. 109-12.

[2] On this practice, see J. Gee, *The Trade and Navigation of Great Britain Considered*, pp. 49-50.

[3] Walpole to Rochford, 4 July 1774, Enclosure N.2, P.R.O. S.P. 89/77. Of the clearances, 19 were for Newfoundland, 27 for Philadelphia, 2 each for Maryland and Virginia, and 1 each for New York and New England.

[4] H.R. (V.N.). Rough Journal, 1761-6, Journal, 1766-9. The firm often arranged the freights for vessels sailing northwards, for which it charged a commission of 2 per cent.

7 *Bullion to England*

THE REMAINING PRINCIPAL branch of Anglo-Portuguese trade consisted of the export of bullion, chiefly gold coin, from Portugal to England, in settlement of Portugal's trading accounts with England and her North American colonies. Supplementing these flows were those arising from the Dutch, German and other European nations' trading surpluses with Portugal. Together they constituted a major branch of business normally far exceeding in value either the foodstuffs or the wine trades.

In some respects bullion was the most attractive of all the commodities exchanged between England and Portugal for merchants to do business in. Highly standardized and indestructible, it had a high value in relation to bulk and was immediately negotiable. But there were two serious drawbacks. In the first place, although silver could be shipped abroad from Portugal under licence, the export of gold was prohibited by a statute of 1325, under pain of death to the offender and confiscation of the gold, the prohibition being lifted only in times of great dearth of corn.[1] The Portuguese government, however, on the whole recognized the undesirability of attempting to enforce this law: in 1716 the English Consul in Lisbon remarked 'the Government here have been all along sensible that the Exportation of their Gold has been and must be unavoidable (they have nothing else wherewith to Balance our Trade)',[2] and in 1760 Pombal openly agreed with the English Envoy on the necessity of not enforcing the law.[3]

[1] B.M. Add. MSS. 23,634, printed in A. R. Walford, *The British Factory in Lisbon*, p. 63; L. S. Sutherland, *A London Merchant*, p. 36n.; *Mercator's Letters on Portugal and its Commerce*, p. 6.

[2] Letter of William Poyntz, 10 March 1716 N.S., attached to Poyntz to Pringle, 18 April 1716, P.R.O. S.P. 89/24.

[3] 'We know . . . well . . . the Sums which Great Britain draws from this Country, but we know too that our Money must go out to pay for what we want for ourselves and our Colonies.' B.M. Add. MSS. 40,760, ff. 89-91. See also, Add. MSS. 23,634, ff. 44, 49, and *Occasional Thoughts on the Portuguese Trade* (1767), pp. 12-13.

Nevertheless, arrests and seizures did occur, chiefly because of the zeal of Customs officers who received part of the confiscated bullion in proven cases. Thus in October 1715, '5000 *Crusados* in Silver & 7000 in Gold' (about £1,590) were seized on board a merchant ship in the Tagus;[1] in September 1721 Ferdinand Wingfield, a leading member of the Lisbon Factory, was temporarily imprisoned and his cash, papers and goods seized, on suspicion of his having exported gold abroad;[2] in March 1734 some '175 pieces of Gold' were seized on board a merchant ship in Lisbon;[3] and in March 1767, 1300 *moedas* (about £1,750) were seized from the mate of the packet-boat *Expedition* at Lisbon as he was preparing to go on board.[4] Such incidents occasioned vigorous English protests, from both the merchant communities and the consular and diplomatic representatives, which helped ensure that short imprisonments only were the worst personal penalties suffered, and that usually, after some delay, seized consignments were restored.[5] The second drawback of the bullion trade was its attractiveness as a subject for robbery both on land and sea. Together these factors shaped business practice in a distinctive fashion.

Throughout the period Lisbon was by far the chief centre for bullion shipments to England. This was assured both by its position as the leading market for English goods in Portugal, and by the great advantage it had over the other Portuguese ports in the availability of highly suitable vessels for bullion carriage to England, that is the Falmouth-Lisbon packet-boats and English men-of-war. The great use made of these vessels meant that Falmouth was the most important bullion importing centre in England, though substantial landings were made at Plymouth, Portsmouth and Chatham in wartime. Probably all the other English ports concerned in the Portuguese

[1] Worsley to Stanhope, 16 November 1715, P.R.O. S.P. 89/23. 'There was much more Money on board, but the Guardsman not having set Guards there the Merchants had time to withdraw all of it before the strictest search was made.'

[2] Worsley to Carteret, 29 September 1721 N.S., P.R.O. S.P. 89/29.

[3] Tyrawly to Newcastle, 17 April 1734, P.R.O. S.P. 89/37.

[4] Hay to Shelburne, 25 March 1767, P.R.O. S.P. 89/63. The dispatches of the English Envoys and Consuls in Portugal preserved in the P.R.O. contain references to at least four other seizures during the period, in 1718, 1752, 1755 and 1761, and there were no doubt other cases.

[5] On two occasions, in 1752 and 1760, the English government backed up protests against seizures by sending special Envoys to Lisbon. Sir Richard Lodge, 'The English Factory at Lisbon', *Transactions of the Royal Historical Society* (1933), pp. 230-1, 237-9.

trade also received some imports, brought in by merchantmen, with London's most likely the largest.

The bullion shipments arising from Anglo-Portuguese trade in the main constituted returns for the merchants in England who chiefly financed English exports to Portugal. Bullion shipments to England were also made on the account of English firms in Portugal as well as North American merchants with balances in Portugal. Bullion was not the only form in which returns could be made from Portugal – the other main ways were in wines, or in bills of exchange drawn on wine importers in England. Since wine importers in England formed generally distinct groups from exporters in England and the English firms in Portugal,[1] the great majority of those wishing to make remittances had the choice of either bills or bullion. The prime factor determining whether bills were bought or whether bullion was shipped, was, as would be expected, the level of the exchange rate between the *milreis* and sterling. When the rate stood above gold export point from Portugal no doubt all remittances were made in bills and, conversely, when the exchange was very low – when bills on England were very expensive – all remittances were made in bullion. The latter seems to have been the case in 1711 when the exchanges turned sharply against the Portuguese: in that year the annual London rate on Lisbon (average of the first-monthly rates) was as low as 5s. 1½d., and no first-monthly rate rose above 5s. 3d., par being about 5s. 7d. and gold export point from Lisbon about 5s. 6d. In October the English Consul in Lisbon observed, '[the goods] & ye vast quantity of Corn wee import returns all in mony again, & tis not easily computed what vast sums goe by every Convoy, nay every packett. The fleet wth Sr John Norris . . . carryed away large sums, several houses sending twenty to forty thousand p^d a house & all some.'[2] Other years of particularly low exchanges when bullion exporting would have been common were 1708 (annual London rate on Lisbon, 5s. 2¼d.), 1712-13 (5s. 3d. and 5s. 3⅝d.), and 1720 (5s. 3⅞d.). In five other years between 1700 and 1770 the annual rate of exchange stood below 5s. 4½d., in 1719, 1721-2, 1726 and 1746. Bullion exporting may have been common in numerous other years through the period when for a month or two the exchanges were very low.

[1] See above, Chapter 5.
[2] Milner to the Lord Treasurer, 19 October 1711, P.R.O. S.P. 89/21.

But when the exchange rate stood at or not much below gold export point from Portugal, as it did for most of the time, the practice of merchants differed radically, some making remittances in bills and others in bullion. This variation in practice sprang from the risks inherent in bullion exporting from Portugal, and in the varying financial abilities of the merchants to meet them. A paper of 1752 by Lord Tyrawly, the English Envoy in Lisbon, indicates that the men with limited capital, for whom the seizure of a parcel of gold could

Table VI CONSIGNEES FOR BULLION SHIPPED ON THE LISBON-FALMOUTH PACKET-BOATS, JANUARY-JUNE 1741

London Exchange Rate on Lisbon, 1741 (shillings and pence)		*Date of Packet's Arrival in Falmouth, 1741*	*Number of Consignees*	*Value of Bullion Shipped* £
2 January	5s. $4\frac{7}{8}$d.	18 January	61	28,844
		30 January	33	18,941
3 February	5s. $4\frac{7}{8}$d.	9 February	24	12,144
3 March	5s. 5d.	21 March	25	11,803
3 April	5s. $5\frac{1}{8}$d.	5 April	18	10,046
		11 April	25	11,226
1 May	5s. $5\frac{1}{2}$d.	7 May	12	5,389
2 June	5s. $5\frac{3}{8}$d.	5 June	13	3,180
		8 June	11	3,291

Sources: J. Castaing, *Course of the Exchange*, and Chol. (H.) MSS. P. 89, 17/1.

cause serious difficulty or even ruin, normally preferred to have their remittances in bills even though it meant a lower return. And that the 'very Rich and Considerable Houses, whether in London or Lisbon', who were better able to withstand occasional losses, preferred running the risks of bullion remission for the financial advantage obtained.[1] Merchants of moderate wealth possibly took an intermediate position which changed with quite small movements in the exchange rate. Some evidence for these differing practices as exchange rates changed is presented in Table VI. As will be seen, in the first half of 1741, as the London rate of exchange on Lisbon moved nearer the gold export point of about 5s. 6d., the number of consignees on the packet-boats, and the value of the bullion shipped, fell away sharply. A further factor influencing whether or not merchants made their remittances in bullion may well have been the place from which the

[1] B.M. Add. MSS. 23,634, ff. 74, 76.

balances were to be remitted. The far less satisfactory opportunities for bullion shipment at Oporto and the other provincial Portugues ports probably led to remitting in bills there at markedly lower exchange rates than at Lisbon. To some extent this was lessened, however, by the practice, at least of Oporto merchants, of requesting correspondents at Lisbon to arrange bullion remittances on their behalf.

The disinclination of the lesser men in Anglo-Portuguese trade to remit from Portugal in bullion when the exchange rate was at or not much below gold export point, led to the rise of bullion dealing by some of the wealthier English merchants in the trade in both countries. Lord Tyrawly's papers of 1752 indicate that the lesser men carried 'their Money to the great Dealers who will Venture it', and in return 'take their Bills' on England, for which 'they must pay the Exchange and in some cases Brokeredge too'.[1] Dealers tried to ensure that the bills of exchange and the bullion travelled together on the packets or men-of-war so that funds were available when the bills fell due for payment – in 1716 the bills were drawn at thirty days' sight.[2] The possibility of the confiscation of a consignment, even if only temporary, or of delays in transit, made the large capital of the dealers imperative. Assistance to this traffic was given by at least one English Envoy in Lisbon who provided a special bag for the merchants' letters and bills of lading so 'that they might not run any risk in having them opened at the Post House'.[3]

Undoubtedly other businessmen, normally outside the trade, also participated in such bullion dealing. The London merchant, William Braund, for example, became a specialist bullion importer from Portugal in 1756, when he effectively ceased exporting woollen goods there, and remained so for the duration of the Seven Years War.[4] In making the change to bullion dealer Braund was much influenced by the gold trade's high profitability in these years, due initially to the weakening of the *milreis* and later to the sharp wartime rise in the London market price of gold. After a slow start his business became quite substantial: at its peak in 1758-61 his annual imports averaged £12,200 and showed little fluctuation. In one major respect his practice

[1] B.M. Add. MSS. 23,634, f. 76, and letter to Holdernesse, 4 June 1752, P.R.O. S.P. 89/48.

[2] See Worsley to Stanhope, 24 February 1716 N.S., P.R.O. S.P. 89/24.

[3] Ibid.

[4] L. S. Sutherland, *A London Merchant*, pp. 22-4, 32-40.

differed from that described above. His Lisbon agents, Jackson, Branfill and Goddard, instead of offering bills of exchange on England, bought bullion with funds obtained from bills drawn on houses in Portugal that Braund sent them from London.[1] The bills were mostly those of London merchants on correspondents: provincial merchants' bills were also used, and 'accommodation' as well as trade bills. The bill brokerage and additional time involved in this method made it rather more costly than that described above.[2] It cannot be shown how widespread or frequent bullion dealing such as Braund's was during the years under study. But the temporary nature of his ventures, and the rather higher costs, suggest it was restricted to a few periods, chiefly in wartime, when bullion importing was especially profitable.

The bullion transfers made to England in settlement of the Dutch, German and other foreign nations' commercial balances with Portugal were similarly organized. Some bullion was shipped by the foreign merchants themselves, but those houses who were unwilling to face the attendant hazards sold their bullion to English dealers: 'Our English Merchants likewise have the Profit of the Exchange for the Exporting Money for the Foreign Nations that Trade at Lisbon who rather Chuse to take English Bills than Venture to Send it [a]way themselves', wrote Lord Tyrawly in 1752.[3] Such dealing in foreign balances was not confined to the great Portugal merchants. In his time as a specialist importer William Braund obtained funds by buying bills of exchange drawn on Portuguese merchants in Lisbon and Oporto by firms in Hamburg, Amsterdam, France and Italy;[4] while in 1754 reference was made to the 'almost . . . daily practice of [the English] buying Bills' for the balances in Portugal belonging to other foreign nations.[5]

Three main kinds of shipping carried the bullion to England – merchant vessels, packet-boats, and warships. At the chief centre of

[1] Some of the early bullion shipments settled outstanding cloth accounts and other debts.

[2] Some calculations made at the latter end of the eighteenth century show that with an intrinsic par of exchange of 5s. 7½d. this method of gold dealing yielded a profit when the London exchange stood at 5s. 5·206d. or below. B.M. Add. MSS. 38,424, f. 155.

[3] B.M. Add. MSS. 23,634, f. 74. See also [N. Magens], *The Universal Merchant* (1753), p. 67.

[4] L. S. Sutherland, op. cit., p. 37.

[5] *Mercator's Letters on Portugal and its Commerce*, p. 37.

shipment, Lisbon, some use was made of merchant vessels returning to England: at the end of the period, in the opinion of the Portuguese, 'allmost all the Merchant Ships employed in the Trade of Lisbon . . . carry different sums of money'.[1] Their employment, however, had serious disadvantages, the possibility of search while in Portuguese waters being the greatest. As normally unarmed vessels too they were vulnerable in peacetime to the Barbary pirates who occasionally menaced the Portuguese coast as far north as the Tagus,[2] while in wartime, when with the added danger of privateers they usually proceeded in convoy, their sailings became far more concentrated together in time and prone to delays.[3] Consequently, in the main, use was made of other, more suitable kinds of shipping. These were, first, the Post Office packet-boats which sailed between Lisbon and Falmouth from the inception of a regular service in 1703. These vessels were highly regarded, since as well as being fast sailers and carrying guns they enjoyed diplomatic immunity from search. Furthermore, although it is unlikely a boat sailed weekly from Lisbon to Falmouth as seems to have been intended, in 1741, 1759-64 and 1769, for which years the number of packets arriving in Falmouth is known, almost invariably one and sometimes two left the Tagus each month.[4] It seems certain that in peacetime the greatest part of the bullion consigned from Lisbon to England was carried by the packet-boats. Their importance can be seen in the alarm expressed by the English Consul and eight of the leading English merchants in Lisbon in February 1716 on the reported ending of the service,[5] and the Consul's comment the following month that 'considerable returns in bullion . . . are every voyage made by them from hence'.[6] Between

[1] Attachment to Lyttelton to Weymouth, 21 June 1769, f. 58, P.R.O. S.P. 89/69.

[2] On this, see Poyntz to Worsley, 18 February 1716 N.S., and Poyntz to Stanhope, 10 March 1716 N.S., P.R.O. S.P. 89/24.

[3] The convoy system is discussed in Chapter 8.

[4] Nine packets entered Falmouth from Lisbon between 18 January and 8 June 1741. Chol. (H.) MSS. P. 89 17/1. In the years 1759-63, 21, 22, 16, 24 and 31 respectively entered Falmouth, one at least arriving every month except in December 1761 and October 1762. In 1764 and 1769 there were 36 and 37 arrivals. The increase in the latter years arose from the use of 5 boats, compared to 4 in 1759-60, 4 (in effect) in 1762-3, and 3 during most of 1761, together with a higher rate of sailings. B.N. Col. Pomb., Cod. 635, ff. 442, 445. In 1703 and again in 1744 the Post Office employed four packets. J. C. Hemmeon, *The History of the British Post Office* (Cambridge, Mass., 1912), pp. 115, 121.

[5] Poyntz to Worsley, 18 February 1716 N.S., P.R.O. S.P. 89/24.

[6] Poyntz to Stanhope, 10 March 1716 N.S., P.R.O. S.P. 89/24. See also *Occasional Thoughts on the Portuguese Trade*, p. 11.

1764 and 1769, in fact, the value of the bullion they annually carried to Falmouth averaged £895,061,[1] which very probably composed the great bulk of total bullion imports into England from Lisbon (including foreign balances) in these years. Undoubtedly, the packets were very important in wartime as well. In the fifteen months from March 1740 to June 1741 their freights amounted to £447,347;[2] in 1757, so the Lisbon Consul was 'credibly informed . . . near One Million and a half Sterling was Ship'd from hence in Specie chiefly on board our Packet boats';[3] and between 1759-63 their average yearly imports into Falmouth came to £680,231.[4] Again, such imports must have constituted a high proportion of Lisbon's trade. The value of the bullion carried by individual packet-boats varied greatly: between 1759 and 1764 it ranged from £1,768 on the *King George* in September 1762, to £71,733 on the *Expedition* in March 1760.[5]

From Lisbon bullion was also shipped on homeward-bound English men-of-war, both frigates and ships of the line. Strongly armed as well as possessing diplomatic immunity from search, they were almost ideal for bullion carriage and it was in fact common for captains to supplement their incomes in this way.[6] In 1758 the English Consul in Lisbon observed 'the Merchants here would allways give preference to Ships of Warr . . . for the Freight of . . . Specie home',[7] and it is unlikely he had only war years in mind. Their superiority to the packets was acknowledged in the higher freight rates they commanded during the Seven Years War, of the order of 1 per cent of the bullion's value[8] compared to the ¼-½ per cent charged by the packets.[9] The prospect of profitable freights to England encouraged

[1] B.N. Col. Pomb., Cod. 635, f. 445; Cod. 636, f. 10.

[2] Chol. (H.) MSS. P. 44, 50; P. 89, 17/1.

[3] Frankland to Pitt, 20 August 1758, P.R.O. S.P. 89/51.

[4] B.N. Col. Pomb., Cod. 635, f. 445. In 1718, a year of minor Anglo-Spanish war, the English Factory in Lisbon said that they remitted 'most of the Gold, the return of our Manufactorys, by the Packet-boats'. Worsley to Craggs, 23 September 1718 N.S., P.R.O. S.P. 89/26.

[5] B.N. Col. Pomb., Cod. 635, f. 445. In mid-1740, when the *Townshend* packet outward from Lisbon was taken by a Spanish privateer of 24 guns some 20 leagues from England, her freight of 'Specie and Gold Barrs' came to 54,665 *milreis* (*c.* £14,800). P.R.O. C.M.E. C.110, 19, 20, Pratt *ex parte*, Hitchcock to Hitchcock, 6 August 1740.

[6] See *Augustus Hervey's Journal*, ed. D. Erskine (1953), *passim*, for an account of the background to such business.

[7] Frankland to Pitt, 20 August 1758, P.R.O. S.P. 89/51.

[8] L. S. Sutherland, op. cit., p. 36.

[9] Ibid., and H.R. (V.N.), Journal 1755-65, entry of 1 October 1756. About 1724, ½ per

warships to enter Lisbon for no other reason, if weight can be placed on Lord Tyrawly's comment that 'there is not an English Man of Warr homeward bound from almost any Point of the Compass that does not take Lisbon in their Way home . . . every Body knows that [they] have no other Business in life here but to carry away Money'.[1] In peacetime, however, the numbers of English men-of-war visiting the Tagus probably remained quite low. In the years 1765-8, for instance, only 5, 7, 5 and 3 respectively are recorded as arriving at Lisbon,[2] while in 1773 only 6 sailed from the port,[3] their destinations not being given. But in war years, especially when Portugal was actively allied to England, their numbers and role in the bullion trade undoubtedly grew strikingly.

Dutch men-of-war too were sometimes used by the Lisbon merchants. In April 1746 certain principal members of the English Factory declared that the weakness of the packets and the great numbers of French privateers had obliged them since hostilities started with France in 1744 to use all available Dutch warships for making bullion remittances.[4] And ten months later Dutch warships were still being used.[5] Whether the bullion first went to England or Holland is not clear, but the former seems more likely. They were again used during the Seven Years War, the merchants preferring them and other neutral warships since unlike English men-of-war they were not liable to attack by privateers.[6]

At Oporto and the other Portuguese ports exporters had to rest content with merchant vessels for the direct carriage of bullion to England,[7] except for the rare occasion when a man-of-war became available.[8] But some provincial remittances in bullion, in the case of Oporto houses at least, were made via Lisbon. In the late 1750s and the 1760s Holdsworth, Olive and Newman regularly sent funds on

cent was generally charged by the packet captains and sometimes $\frac{1}{3}$ per cent. Letter initialled 'W', 5 September 1724, P.R.O. S.P. 100/39.

[1] Tyrawly to Newcastle, 29 September 1734, P.R.O. S.P. 89/37, and 7 January 1741, P.R.O. S.P. 89/40.

[2] Attachments 1-4, Lyttelton to Weymouth, 13 March 1769, P.R.O. S.P. 89/67.

[3] Enclosure N.2, Walpole to Rochford, 4 July 1774, P.R.O. S.P. 89/77.

[4] Attachment to Castres to Newcastle, 17 April 1746, P.R.O. S.P. 89/44.

[5] Castres to Keene, 13 February 1747, P.R.O. S.P. 89/46.

[6] *Occasional Thoughts on the Portuguese Trade*, p. 11.

[7] On the use of merchant vessels at Oporto, see attachment to Lyttelton to Weymouth, 21 June 1769, f. 58, P.R.O. S.P. 89/69.

[8] In April 1759 Holdsworth, Olive and Newman of Oporto wrote to one of their

their own account or on the account of merchants in England to their Lisbon correspondent, Christopher Hake, for shipment in bullion to England by either packet-boats or warships.[1] During the Seven Years War their instructions sometimes revealed a strong preference for warships. In December 1759 Hake was asked to remit 2,000 *milreis* (about £540) to England 'if per Packet 500 *milreis* in each, if per M[an] of War 1,000 *milreis* each';[2] and in April 1760 they wanted 1,200 *milreis* remitted in the *Windsor* man-of-war but if she had sailed 600 *milreis* only on 'a Packet [which] goes soon'.[3] Hake's commission for his services was ½ per cent.

The English merchants' conduct of their bullion shipping at Lisbon was not always as discreet as its riskiness warranted. In 1734, for example, the English Envoy in Lisbon roundly criticized 'the Merchants [who] talk as publicly upon the Exchange of what Money they have Shipped for England, and with as little Secresie send it on board, as they do a Chest of Oranges'.[4] At times, too, the English representatives in Lisbon complained of the difficulties caused them, and the heightening of the popular obloquy attaching to the English for exporting bullion, by exaggerated English newspaper reports of shipments from Portugal. In 1716 'the Portuguese Gazette printed in this City' reprinted an English report that the *Gibraltar* man-of-war had carried to England £200,000 in gold: this was 'about ten times as much as She really had on board', remarked the English Consul, who thought 'it would be extremely convenient that strict orders

principal Dartmouth consignors, 'should have remitted you something considerable ere this on Acct of Walley's Cargoe but have not had an opportunity. We have been waiting for a good Convoy from hence but there is no other than a Sloop of 10 Guns, & she will have 40 ships wth her so we are afraid to Venture anything by her.' A further reason for not shipping bullion was the rising exchange: 'the Ex[change] is now at 5/6¾ and will be 67d. We will remitt you in good bills soon . . .' H.R. (V.N.). Letter Book, Dec. 1758-Oct. 1760, letter to Thos. Holdsworth, 20 April 1759. As noted above, Chapter 1, p. 21n., exchange rates in Portugal were generally above those in England. The high rate of exchange for gold exporting would have been due to the rise in the London price of gold. See Appendix VII.

[1] H.R. (V.N.). Journal, 1755-65; Current Account Book, 1755-60; Letter Books, Dec. 1758-Oct. 1760 and Oct. 1760-Nov. 1765, *passim*.

[2] Ibid., Letter Book, Dec. 1758-Oct. 1760, letter to C. Hake, 15 December 1759.

[3] Ibid., letter to C. Hake, 26 April 1760.

[4] Tyrawly to Newcastle, 17 April 1734, P.R.O. S.P. 89/37. 'The Portuguese cannot be Ignorant of what Gold is sent out by the least attention to our Conduct, since the Bills of Lading to send it home either by the Packets or Men of War, are generally signed at the Publick Coffee House.' Lord Tyrawly writing in 1755, B.M. Add. MSS. 23,634, printed in A. R. Walford, *The British Factory in Lisbon*, p. 64.

were given to all the printers and writers of our News Papers that they would forbear mentioning anything of that nature for ye future'.[1]

Undoubtedly the great bulk of the bullion shipped to England was destined for London, for the account of both English and foreign merchants or their agents there. Part of the merchantmen's cargoes probably went directly there, while occasionally a man-of-war with a parcel of bullion on board might sail up the Thames. But normally the warships came no nearer than Chatham, and often ended their voyages at Portsmouth or Plymouth, while the bullion freighted on the packet-boats was all landed at Falmouth. In consequence, certain further transfer problems must have arisen. In the case of the Falmouth landings some London merchants evidently preferred their imports remitted in inland bills of exchange which their Cornish agents were instructed to purchase with the bullion itself.[2] Such instructions clearly caused considerable strain in the local bill market. In 1737 the Receiver-General of Taxes for Cornwall complained that ever since the re-establishment of credit following the South Sea crisis all the bills in the county had been engrossed in this way.[3] The bill supply generally proved quite inadequate for the very large remittances involved, and the bulk of the bullion was sent overland to London by carrier. Between January and June 1741, for example, of the packets' bullion freights worth £104,863, all, except for £5,176 delivered to merchants and others in the West Country, was carried to London.[4] In early 1723 the carriage charge fell from ½ per cent of the value to ⅜ per cent:[5] in 1735 it was still ⅜ per cent.[6] In February 1723, following the theft of 2,000 *moedas* (about £2,750) by a carrier's servant, sixty-six London merchants contracted with John Goodall of Fowey for

[1] Letter of William Poyntz, 10 March 1716 N.S., attached to Poyntz to Pringle, 18 April 1716, P.R.O. S.P. 89/24. And in 1738, Lord Tyrawly, without doubt the most trenchant of the English Envoys at Lisbon during the period, delivered the following broadside. 'It is a most Miserable thing, that there is no Stopping the Mouths of Our News Writers. These Paragraphs . . . do us infinite hurt. They set down the Gold they hear or dream We extract from Portugal, with just [as] little Caution as they do the Oats and Barley that are sold at Bear-Key. If those People could be confined to the Accounts of High Way Men, and Horses stolen or strayed, their Papers would be every bit as diverting and instructive to the Generality of their Readers.' Tyrawly to Newcastle, 22 August 1738, P.R.O. S.P. 89/40.

[2] *Cal. Treas. Books and Papers*, 1735-8, p. 315.

[3] Ibid., p. 314.

[4] Chol. (H.) MSS. P. 89, 17/1.

[5] Letter initialled 'W', 5 September 1724, P.R.O. S.P. 100/39.

[6] *Cal. Treas. Books and Papers*, 1735-8, p. 315.

the carriage of their bullion imported into Falmouth.[1] Probably most of the bullion landed at Chatham and the other naval bases for London merchants was also carried overland to London. In October 1711, a time of pressure on the coin supply in the country, the Bank of England offered to bring bullion to London from the men-of-war 'from Lisbon that shall come into the River or to Chatham' for any person who presented the bills of lading.[2] It cannot be shown how far the bullion remitted to provincial merchants was shipped directly to them, but many probably had their imports brought to London and handled by agents there.

Merchants could dispose of their imports in a number of ways. First, since they mostly consisted of Portuguese coin – mainly gold *moedas* but also silver *crusados* – which could circulate freely in England and was generally acceptable, they could be used as cash. Second, imports could be sold to, or deposited with, the London or country banks (excluding here the Bank of England). Probably both methods were much resorted to. For during most if not all of the period under study, Portuguese coin was widely current in England. It was particularly common in the West of England, as would be expected: in 1713 an Exeter man wrote 'we have hardly any other Money current among us but Portuguese gold',[3] while in 1737 it was stated 'for many years past very little specie of any other kind' circulated in Cornwall.[4] Its circulation was wider however. In 1742 the single, double and quadruple *moedas* were called 'in great measure the current coin of the Kingdom';[5] about 1750 an 'immense quantity' of Portuguese gold coin was stated to be in circulation;[6] and in 1757 it was declared as plentiful as ever.[7] This coin came to England from many places, from

[1] 'Case of the Portugal Merchants' [20 August 1724], and 'Agreement of several London Merchants with Mr. Goodall', P.R.O. S.P. 100/39.

[2] B. of E. Court Book F, f. 177. See also ff. 220, 235, cited by Sir John Clapham, *The Bank of England. A History* (Cambridge, 1944), Vol. I, p. 134.

[3] C. King (ed.), *The British Merchant*, Vol. II, p. 24.

[4] *Cal. Treas. Books and Papers*, 1735-8, p. 315. Portuguese gold coin comprised nearly all the tax monies collected by the Cornish Receiver-General at that time. Ibid., p. 314.

[5] The Rev. Peter Vallavine, *Observations on the Present Condition of the Current Coin of the Kingdom* (1742), quoted by Sir John Craig, *The Mint* (Cambridge, 1953), p. 240.

[6] Isaac de Pinto, *An Essay on Circulation and Credit* (1774), p. 65, translator's note.

[7] Corbyn Morris, *Letter to Lord Powis on the Causes of the Present State of our Silver Coin* (1757), quoted by Sir John Craig, op. cit. pp. 240-1. Before 1714 the Treasury officially valued the *moeda* at 28s. and thereafter at 27s. 6d. Ibid., p. 215. See also *Occasional Thoughts on the Portuguese Trade* (1767), p. 38.

the Continent, Ireland and the West Indies,[1] but undoubtedly most came directly from Portugal and largely on the account of the Portugal merchants. It must, therefore, to a great extent, have been initially put into circulation either by the merchants, or by institutions who bought gold from them and used it as cash. Such institutions were principally the private banks which accepted and made payments in Portuguese coin in their daily business, unlike the Bank of England which passed on all the foreign coin it received to the Mint for recoining or reserved it for use in international transactions.[2] A third way of disposing of imports was by sale to goldsmiths and other bullion dealers.

Importers could also sell their bullion directly to the Bank of England. Some evidence for the early years of the century suggests such transactions then may have been notable. Of fifteen London merchants trading to Portugal who drew up a memorial in June 1711,[3] the Bank's records show that five sold gold to the Bank between February 1711 and February 1712. They were John Ward, James Milner, Samuel Clarke, Sir John Houblon and Peter Delmé. Their individual sales were £3,497, £24,880, £12,188, £2,435 and £6,172 respectively, totalling £49,170 or 20 per cent of the Bank's total purchases of £247,653.[4] Part of the gold sold, particularly in Milner's case, may have come from bullion dealing, or from other sources than the Portuguese trade. At this time, as well as purchasing gold, the Bank also offered advances on gold deposited with it, and Ward, Clarke and Houblon all received loans on this basis.[5] Four of the five men were among the leading Portugal merchants of the time,[6] and three, Ward, Houblon and Delmé, were directors of the Bank in

[1] See ibid., pp. 38-9, and Sir John Clapham, op. cit., Vol. I, p. 136.

[2] On the practices of the private banks and the Bank of England concerning Portuguese coin, see Isaac de Pinto, op. cit., p. 66, translator's note, and Sir John Clapham, op. cit., pp. 133-4, 136.

[3] P.R.O. C.O. 389/22, f. 194.

[4] B. of E., General Ledger IV, ff. 513, 571, 647, 655. Although some names in the Bank's ledger lack initials it is virtually certain the same men were involved.

[5] Ibid., ff. 571, 647, 655. For an account of the Bank's bullion dealings to 1764 see, Sir John Clapham, op. cit., pp. 131-41.

[6] Between 1713 and 1715 the Commissioners for Trade called on Ward, Clarke, Delmé and a 'Mr. Milner', probably James Milner, as leading Portugal merchants, among others, to attend them for consultation. *Journal of Trade*, 1708-9 to 1714-15, pp. 482-3, 533-4, 543, 608-9. Sir John Houblon had died in January 1712.

the year concerned.[1] Altogether another thirty-three men sold gold to the Bank in this period, and it is more than likely that some were merchants trading to Portugal or agents acting for them. In May 1727 another London Portugal merchants' memorial had fifty-three names appended:[2] of these only David Bosanquet and Henry Gaultier appeared among the Bank's gold suppliers in 1727, with sales of £1,800 and £1,370 respectively, the Bank's total purchases amounting to £261,084.[3] The main reason for this change is probably found in the increasing specialization of the London bullion market during the intervening fifteen years, under the stimulus of a regular and generally expanding bullion trade. Such important Portugal merchants as John Barnard, Samuel Clarke, and Peter Burrell, now probably found it more convenient to sell their imports to specialist bankers and dealers, who in turn supplied the Bank to a greater extent than previously. Significantly enough, the Bank's suppliers had fallen sharply from thirty-eight in 1711-12 to fourteen in 1727, although the volume of business remained roughly the same. A further reason may have been that none of the known Portugal merchants of 1727 were directors of the Bank: this former close connection had, if only temporarily, been broken.[4]

Finally, importers of bullion from Portugal could dispose of their bullion by exporting it. No doubt this was done by the foreign merchants who brought bullion into England from Portugal; it was certainly practised by English merchants and bullion dealers in the trade. Anderson, in referring to the Dutch trade balances in Portugal which were remitted by English merchants in bullion to London, remarked that from thence 'the Treasure [was] transmitted to Holland'.[5] And between 1758 and 1761, William Braund, during his time as a specialist bullion importer from Portugal, made five shipments of bullion, mainly gold, to the value of £3,831, to Clifford and

[1] W. Marston Acres, *The Bank of England from Within, 1694-1900* (1931), Vol. II, pp. 613-14.

[2] P.R.O. S.P. 100/39, f. 187.

[3] B. of E. General Ledger VIII, ff. 88-9. This is the latest date for this purpose as soon after the Bank's records lose their personal character.

[4] Only John Page and John Ward (not to be confused with Sir John Ward) had previously been directors. W. Marston Acres, op. cit., pp. 614-15.

[5] A. Anderson, *An Historical Deduction of the Origin of Commerce*, Vol. I, Introduction, p. x.

Sons, the Amsterdam bankers. The shipments were made in Dutch or English men-of-war.[1]

The bullion trade, then, because of its unique features, exhibited a quite distinctive organization, in terms not only of the ports and shipping resorted to and in the disposal of the product, but in the way in which for much of the time the transfers between England and Portugal tended to be handled very largely by the larger merchants alone.

Thus it will be seen that commercial organization in the four main constituent branches of Anglo-Portuguese trade while possessing much in common also showed some marked variations. In general, the trade was chiefly conducted between London, Lisbon and Oporto, although other ports in both countries were actively engaged, notably in the foodstuffs, wine and bullion trades. English merchants in England largely controlled and financed the business done, although from the 1730s onwards English merchant houses in Portugal and, in the 1760s, English colonial-American merchants became increasingly involved. The extent of commercial investment varied with the branch of business, but at the trade's height in the late 1750s the total sums involved had reached very considerable proportions. In the textile trade merchants generally traded on their own account, but where in addition to capital needs the element of risk was high or where special expertise and close personal supervision was necessary, as in the foodstuffs and wine trades, then a significant resort was made to joint ventures or other ways of sharing financial involvement. In the same way as the commercial investment demanded by the trade was almost entirely met by English and colonial-American merchants, so too was the capital embodied in the shipping that serviced the trade, English and colonial-American owned. Anglo-Portuguese trade demonstrates well the high degree of refinement reached in the organization of English overseas trade by the early eighteenth century, and the existence of well-developed commercial ties binding many parts of England with distant consumers and producers.

[1] L. S. Sutherland, *A London Merchant*, p. 38.

THE PATTERN OF FLUCTUATIONS

8 *Seasonal and Yearly Fluctuations*

THE FIRST TWO chapters of this study were concerned with the long-term growth and subsequent decline of Anglo-Portuguese trade between 1700 and 1770: this chapter examines the short-term changes in the volume of transactions, both seasonal and yearly. Such fluctuations were quite marked. They stemmed essentially from variations in agricultural activity whether in England, Portugal or Brazil – that is from agriculture both as a source of output and as a source of incomes – and from variations in the output of the Brazilian mines. But there were other causes, notably the timing of the Portuguese trading fleets to and from Brazil and the effects of war.

As far as the flows of transactions from season to season are concerned, activity in the England-Portugal trade was fairly well distributed, although the outward trade from England was rather busier in the latter half of the year. In the textiles trade shipments were made throughout the year, but were normally heaviest between June and October with a second, if lesser, busy period about February.[1] Metropolitan demand was at its height in the late summer and autumn after the harvests had exerted their stimulating effect on employment and incomes. The period of buoyancy was extended by the time-spread of the Portuguese harvests: in the central and southern provinces, wheat, the chief crop, was normally cut between May and July; in the north the staple crop, maize, was harvested rather later, in August and September; while the wine vintages were usually held in September or October. Although metropolitan sales fell away in the winter

[1] In 1711 the Oporto Factory indicated August and March as the two 'proper Seasons for the Ships getting in and for the Expense of our Commodities'. Representation of 30 August 1711, P.R.O. C.O. 388/15, M.122.

months, business was very well maintained by the needs of the Lisbon merchants fitting out the fleets for Brazil. These were scheduled to depart for Pernambuco in November, for Rio de Janeiro in January and for Pará and Maranhão in March.[1] With the spring, with its further round of agricultural payments and the general holding of fairs, metropolitan demands again revived for a time.

In the wine and foodstuffs trades the timing of production too was crucial, although by no means the only influential factor. In the Lisbon wine trade, where the wines shipped were mostly of the last vintage, shipment occurred mainly in November and the months immediately following. But at Oporto, where until about 1740 the wines shipped were also predominantly of the last vintage, the busiest season was usually not until March and the months following, after the ending of the winter floods on the river Douro had enabled the wines to be brought safely down-river. After 1740, when Oporto's shipments mostly consisted of older wines, a more extended shipping period from April to the end of the year had become usual.[2] If the Lisbon and Oporto trades are seen together, then wine shipping from Portugal occurred fairly steadily throughout the year, Lisbon's activity in the early months compensating for Oporto's quietness at that time.

In the cod trade from North America a regular seasonal pattern existed, dictated by the fishing season which lasted from May to November, so that the bulk of the catch reached Portugal in the latter months of the year. This can be seen, for 1767-70, in Table VII.

In the grainstuffs trades from England, shipments were more irregular, as can be seen in Table VIII.

[1] J. de Macedo, *A Situação Económica no Tempo de Pombal*, p. 166. It is not clear when the Bahia fleet was scheduled to sail. The Lisbon Factory in 1715 declared that the weeks preceding a fleet's departure were 'the chief season for the expence of our Woolen manufactories'. Memorial of 19 June 1715, P.R.O. C.O. 388/20, P. 71. In April 1722 the English Consul in Lisbon reported that 'on the 4th instant nineteen Ships . . . sailed from this Harbour for the Bahia . . . Our Merchants say . . . that the Demand for Goods, especially those of the English Manufacture, they scarce ever knew so great as it has of late been.' Lumley to Carteret, April 1722 N.S., P.R.O. S.P. 89/30.

[2] Between September 1767 and August 1768 Holdsworth, Olive and Newman's shipment of 252 pipes from Oporto was distributed as follows, by percentages: January-March, 5; April-June, 28; July-September, 31; October-December, 36. H.R. (V.N.). Rough Book, 1766-9. In 1779-80 Offley, Campion and Brooks' much greater shipments, averaging 4,371 pipes annually, were respectively distributed over the same periods, as follows (in percentages): 3, 52, 31, and 14. O.F. (V.N.). Journal and Waste Books, 1779-85.

Table VII COD SHIPS FROM NORTH AMERICA UNLOADING IN OPORTO, 1767-1770

	1767-8	1768-9	1769-70	*Total*
August	0	0	1	1
September	2	4	7	13
October	1	3	11	15
November	7	14	0	21
December	10	0	4	14
January	0	0	0	0
February	1	6	0	7
March	3	0	0	3
	—	—	—	—
	24	27	23	74

Source: H.R. (V.N.). Tables in Rough Book, 1766-9.

Merchants' decisions to ship grain to Portugal depended on an apparent margin of profit between English and Portuguese grain prices (with the export bounty, freight rates and other items taken into account), and would have responded fairly closely to its increase or decrease. Variations in harvest yields and stock positions in the two countries, produced changes, sometimes marked changes, in English and Portuguese prices during the course of all years and from one year to another.[1] In consequence profit margins must have varied

Table VIII LADINGS OF WHEAT IN LONDON FOR PORTUGAL, 1764-1765 (PERCENTAGES)

	Jan.- March	*Apr.- June*	*July- Sept.*	*Oct.- Dec.*	*Total Ladings (quarters)*
1764	22	41	21	16	65,999
1765	15	3	15	67	40,227

Source: T. de T., M. dos N.E., Maço 6, Nos. 45-8.

[1] The London wheat prices listed twice-weekly from 1738 by John Castaing, *Course of the Exchange*, varied in all years and from one year to another, and the variations in the Michaelmas prices of wheat at Cambridge from 1704, T. S. Ashton, *An Economic History of England: the 18th Century*, p. 239, strongly suggest this applied before 1738. Weekly or monthly prices for Lisbon and Oporto are lacking, but monthly wheat prices from 1737 for Evora, an important market in the Alentejo about 70 miles south-east of Lisbon, V. Magalhães Godinho, *Prix et Monnaies au Portugal*, pp. 113-25, behaved similarly and were probably typical of other markets, while Lisbon August wheat prices from 1728 and Oporto *prix courants de l'année* for wheat from 1740, ibid., pp. 76-7, 81-2 also changed, sometimes markedly, from year to year.

significantly during the course of most years in the period, and also from year to year.

In the transfer of bullion from Portugal to England, the distribution of business by season can be shown for two years.

Table IX DISTRIBUTION OF BULLION IMPORTS ON THE FALMOUTH PACKETS, 1764 AND 1769 (PERCENTAGES BY VALUE)

	Jan.- March	*Apr.- June*	*July- Sept.*	*Oct.- Dec.*	*Total Imports* £
1764	20	33	20	27	1,186,714
1769	18	40	24	18	902,456

Source: B.N. Col. Pomb., Cod. 635, ff. 442, 449.

Such a pattern, of a broad distribution of business but with the first half of the year rather more important than the latter half, may well have been typical. Seasonal variations in bullion shipments basically arose from seasonal variations in the flow of commercial payments between England and Portugal. The flow was normally against Portugal throughout the year, but tended to be most adverse in the first half. Remittances for the English textiles sold for the Portuguese domestic market were usually greatest in the early new year and spring, some three to six months after the peak sale period, and this very likely applied to the similar remittances made via England on Dutch and other foreign accounts. While the return of the Brazil fleets and the consequent heavy remittances to England for the English and foreign goods sold for the colonial market, seem to have occurred most often in the latter end of the year and the early months of the new year.[1] Remittances for English grain shipments, however, were irregularly dispersed in accord with the trade's irregularity. The pressure on the *milreis* brought about by these payment flows was in part compensated by the bills of exchange drawn by wine shippers in Portugal on merchants in England at the time the wines were shipped. But since wines were shipped fairly steadily through the year, the compensating effect was spread over the year. These views are borne out by reference to the foreign

[1] This is the impression given by the reports of the Brazil fleets' arrivals contained in the official English dispatches from Portugal. P.R.O. S.P. 89/16-92, *passim*. It is as expected, the fleets being scheduled to complete their round voyages within a year.

exchanges. The first-monthly London rates on Lisbon varied notably during the course of virtually all years in the period, indicating monthly variations in the flow of payments and consequently in bullion shipments. But when the first-monthly rates of exchange are averaged on a quarterly basis for periods of years, as shown in Table X, no marked seasonal differences emerge, although the rates tend to be slightly lower in the first two quarters of the year.

Table X AVERAGE QUARTERLY LONDON RATE OF EXCHANGE ON LISBON, 1700-1770 (IN SHILLINGS AND PENCE PER MILREIS)

	Jan.-March	*Apr.-June*	*July-Sept.*	*Oct.-Dec.*
1701-20	5s. 6½d.	5s. 6¼d.	5s. 6⅝d.	5s. 6⅛d.
1721-40	5s. 5¼d.	5s. 5⅜d.	5s. 5½d.	5s. 5⅜d.
1741-60	5s. 5⅛d.	5s. 5¼d.	5s. 5⅜d.	5s. 5⅜d.
1761-70	5s. 5⅞d.	5s. 6⅜d.	5s. 6⅝d.	5s. 6½d.

Source: J. Castaing, *Course of the Exchange.*

As far as annual fluctuations in the flows of Anglo-Portuguese trade are concerned, these can be broadly indicated by using the official English trade figures and calculating from them the extent to which, year by year, the levels of business deviated from the trend.[1] Figure 3 shows the outcome of such calculations for the total trade flows between the two countries (excluding bullion imports into England). In exports from England the annual deviations from trend averaged 13·3 per cent, and in imports into England, 15·1 per cent. In both exports and imports short-term movements up and down occurred. From low-point to low-point 16 complete movements can be distinguished in exports to Portugal, 13 of three or four years' duration;[2] and 18 movements in the import trade, 13 also of three or four years.[3] Of the three movements in English exports to Portugal longer than four years, 1734-40, 1744-9 and 1758-63, all fell wholly

[1] An eleven-year moving average was considered most suitable for revealing fluctuations, since this typically spanned three of the short-term movements up and down which, as will be seen, characterized the trade. The trends therefore are such as to be influenced as little as possible by the state of the movements up and down, hence making differences from them fully meaningful.

[2] The full distribution was 9 of three years, 4 of four, 2 of five, and 1 of six years. The average duration was 3·7 years.

[3] The full distribution was 3 of two years, 7 of three, 6 of four, 1 of five, and 1 of six years, with an average duration of 3·4 years. In two cases in exports, 1718-21 and 1721-4, and three in imports, 1710-13, 1713-16 and 1716-20, the movements distinguished from

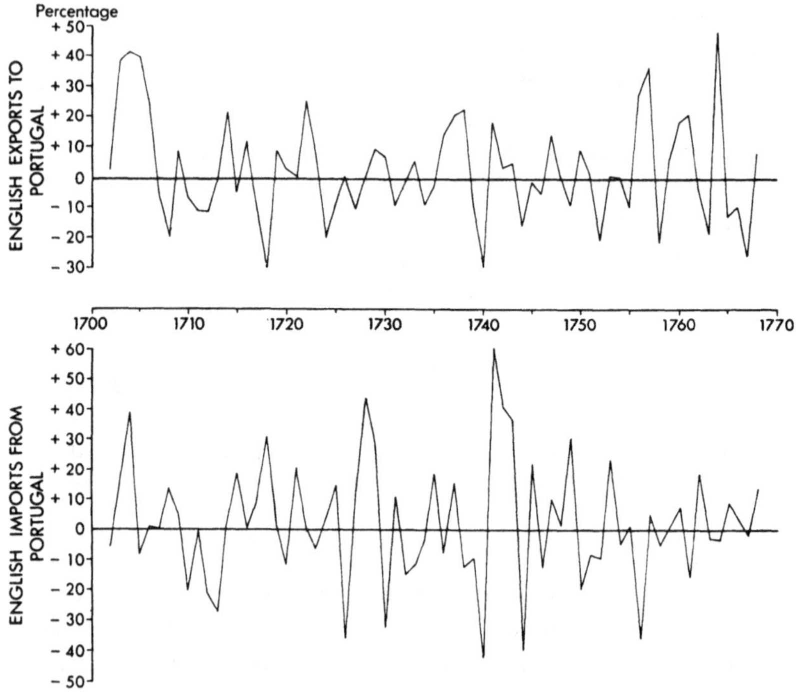

FIGURE 3. Volume of English exports to and imports from Portugal, 1702-1768. Annual percentage deviation from trend (eleven-year geometric moving average). Derived from data in Appendix I.

or partly within periods of Anglo-French and/or Anglo-Spanish war, as did one of the two longer movements in imports into England, 1705-10. With an annual deviation from trend of 20 per cent or over taken to indicate a year of boom or slump in trade, the following emerges (Table XI). The frequent association of major fluctuations with wartime will be noted. Fluctuations in exports and imports showed little correspondence, booms coinciding only in 1704 and slumps in 1740, while in only 33 of 66 years did both trades move in the same direction, again mostly in wartime. The fewer slump years than boom years in exports from England – 5 to 12 – compared to imports into England – 8 to 11 – is explained by the strong upward trend of exports for most of the period.

low-point to low-point do not lie completely around the trend but mostly above or below. Their general character, however, justifies their inclusion. One or two similar cases occur in the branches of trade considered below.

Table XI BOOMS AND SLUMPS IN ENGLISH EXPORTS TO, AND IMPORTS FROM, PORTUGAL, 1700-1770

Booms		*Slumps*	
Exports	*Imports*	*Exports*	*Imports*
1703-6	1704	1718	1710
1714	1718	1740	1712-13
1722	1721	1752	1726
1737-8	1728-9	1758	1730
1756-7	1741-3	1767	1740
1761	1745		1744
1764	1749		1756
	1753		

Source: C. Whitworth, *State of the Trade of Great Britain*, Part II, pp. 27-8.

The pattern of annual fluctuations in the textiles trade and in wheat exports from England can be seen in Figures 4 and 5, while annual fluctuations in wine shipments are portrayed in Figure 6. In the textiles trade the average annual deviation from trend was 15·2 per cent: there were 18 short-term movements up and down, from low-point to low-point, 9 of three years' duration and 3 each of two and four years' duration. In the wine trade the average annual deviation from trend was 14·9 per cent, and there were 17 movements up and down, 9 of four years and 4 of two years. In both trades the association of extremes of business with war years is striking. In the grain trade a strongly patterned movement of business is apparent, though of a marked irregularity.[1] An impression of the way bullion transfers from England to Portugal fluctuated can be seen in the annual totals of bullion carried by the packet-boats in the years 1764-9.[2]

Annual fluctuations in textile, wine and grain shipments all sprang essentially from variations in production, whether in agricultural activity in Portugal, Brazil or England, or in mining activity in Brazil. In the textiles trade the levels of production in Portugal and Brazil were the key factors. Abundant harvests in Portugal meant buoyant employment and incomes in the countryside, and greater prosperity in the towns through lower food prices. In such years the demand for

[1] Wheat exports in 1705, 1712 and 1727 are excluded from Figure 5, because the P.R.O. Customs 3 ledgers for these years are missing.

[2] See above, Chapter 2, p. 45. It is not clear what the trend of transfers was in these years. The English trade surplus was declining, but the growth of colonial-American remittances to England, and the repatriation of English capital from Portugal, may have compensated this decline.

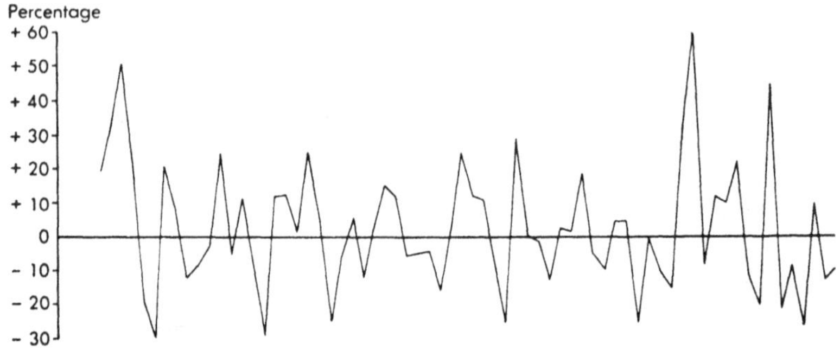

FIGURE 4. Volume of English textiles exported to Portugal, 1703-1770. Annual percentage deviation from trend (eleven-year geometric moving average). After the official values from P.R.O. Customs 3. The textiles included are listed in Appendix III.

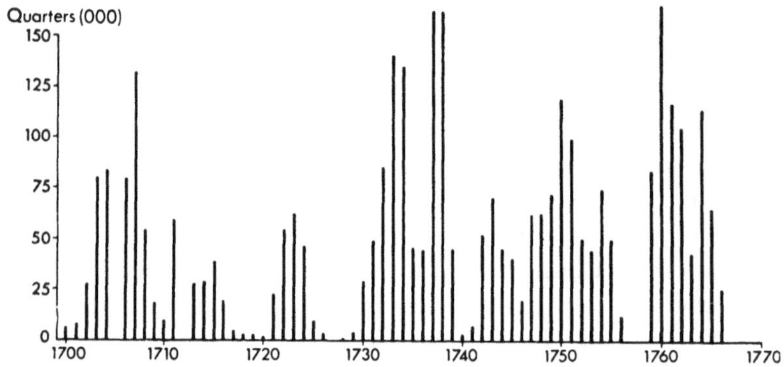

FIGURE 5. Volume of English wheat exports to Portugal, 1700-1766. After the official figures from P.R.O. Customs 3.

English textiles was high: as an Englishman in Portugal remarked, 'a good Crop of Corn in the Kingdom increases the Consumption of Woollen Goods for that Year'.[1] Moreover, when the value of Brazilian output and trade was high,[2] the colony's effective demand for English textiles was also high: this too was, in part, realized by the Englishman

[1] Walpole to Rochford, 4 July 1774, Attachment C, P.R.O. S.P. 89/77.

[2] Magalhães Godinho's figures of gold imports into Lisbon from Brazil, which cover much of the period, show some distinct annual fluctuations, V. M. Godinho, *Annales* (1950), pp. 192-6, as does the yield of the *quinto*, the royal tax on the gold mines, from 1751, V. M. Carnaxide, op. cit., quoted by J. de Macedo, *A Situação Económica no Tempo de Pombal*, p. 183, and also figures of activity in the smelting houses of Minas Gerais and the mint at Villa Rica between 1725 and 1734, C. R. Boxer, *The Golden Age of Brazil*, Appendix IIIa. Brazilian sugar and tobacco output would have fluctuated too.

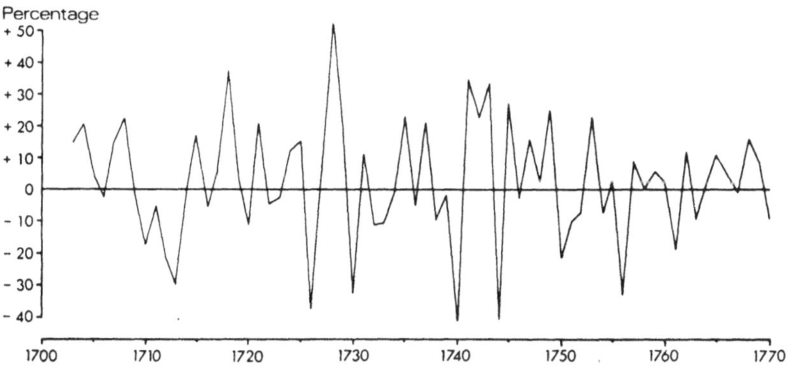

FIGURE 6. Volume of wines imported from Portugal, 1703-1770. Annual percentage deviation from trend (eleven-year geometric moving average). After the official tunnage figures from P.R.O. Customs 3.

just cited when he remarked that 'the quantity of Gold brought from the Mines [to Portugal] influences greatly the Demand of Goods for the Brasils'.[1] English textile sales for Brazil further fluctuated through the confining, until 1765, of the trade with Brazil into four annual fleets which, as noted before, were subject to delays in their sailing, and more important, sometimes sailed to particular regions only biennially.[2]

Fluctuations in English textile exports to Portugal were also institutional in nature. The frequent short-term movements up and down, chiefly every three or four years, indicate the presence of an 'inventory cycle', similar to the four-year movement characterizing English exports in the first half of the nineteenth century.[3] This arose from the difficulty exporting merchants in England had in judging markets accurately. When stocks of textiles in Lisbon and Oporto grew low, factors' reports grew optimistic, and exporters, more or less as one, increased the size of their shipments. Their combined action sooner or later reversed the stock position in Portugal. But this could not be fully appreciated or reported at once to the merchants in England, nor could the merchants' immediate export decisions, nor the orders placed with suppliers and textile producers, be instantaneously reversed. In consequence, more time elapsed before the

[1] Walpole to Rochford, 4 July 1774, Attachment C, P.R.O. S.P. 89/77.
[2] See Chapter 3, p. 58.
[3] W. W. Rostow, *British Economy of the Nineteenth Century* (Oxford, 1948), pp. 36-41.

size of shipments from England declined. As time passed and the level of stocks in Portugal began again to fall, so the conditions for a further 'cycle' appeared.

In the wine trade, yearly fluctuations primarily arose from output and quality differences between vintages. In years of little rain, wine output tended to be low:[1] conversely, in the wetter years the vintages were often abundant, but might be of poorer quality. As the Oporto Factory explained 'the Vintage one Year [is] sometimes double or more than another. [With] the additional Quantity in Wet Years when the Grapes are full of Water, the Quality of consequence must be inferior.'[2] Such variations led to variations in the stocks and prices of the wines purchased by the shippers, and the prices charged merchants in England. The correspondence of John Hitchcock, the Oporto wine shipper, shows this well for the upper Douro vintages of 1738-40. The '38 vintage was average, in both quantity and quality, and by mid-March 1739 Hitchcock had bought some 570 pipes, at an average cost of about 23 *milreis* per pipe;[3] a little later he considered the general shipping price of the Oporto Factory would be about 42 *milreis*.[4] In contrast, the '39 vintage was 'very short' in quantity,[5] and by early April 1740 Hitchcock had still bought only about 200 pipes of red wines;[6] by June his costs averaged over 30 *milreis* per pipe,[7] while general shipping prices had risen to between 47 and 50 *milreis*.[8] In further contrast, the '40 vintage proved abundant but of greatly varying quality. As early as late December Hitchcock had bought 'upwards' of 400 pipes,[9] and by early January 1741 his purchases totalled about 800 pipes, at an unrecorded but evidently lower cost than the previous year: at the same time members of the Oporto Factory were informing merchants in England of shipping

[1] In July 1753 the English Consul in Lisbon lamented, 'the season has been dry soe long, noe moisture in the ground and the grapes begin to fall off'. Letter of G. Crowle, 25 July 1753, P.R.O. S.P. 89/49.

[2] Memorial of 30 April 1765, P.R.O. C.O. 388/53, Ll. 24, No. 23.

[3] P.R.O. C.M.E. C.110 19, 20, Pratt *ex parte*. Hitchcock to Hitchcock, 19 March 1739. In the years 1739-41 the *milreis* on average was worth about 5s. 5d.

[4] Ibid., 11 April 1739.

[5] Ibid., 12 December 1739.

[6] Ibid., 2 April 1740.

[7] Ibid., 11 June 1740.

[8] Ibid., 18 June 1740.

[9] Ibid., 24 December 1740.

prices of 46 to 46·5 *milreis*.[1] When the stocks purchased by shippers were expensive and limited, the orders of merchants in England for wines tended to fall away. And conversely when shippers' stocks were cheap and abundant. Far less important as a cause of fluctuations in the wine trade were changes in the general level of English demand. These would have occurred, to a small extent only in most years, with changes in the general prosperity of the country. By affecting the turnover of merchants' stocks it also affected their willingness to import. Variations in the annual volume of English grain shipments to Portugal sprang from the variations that occurred in profit margins in the trade, brought about by changes in the output and prices of grainstuffs in the two countries, as has already been discussed.

During the Anglo-French and Anglo-Spanish wars of the period the levels of business between England and Portugal were affected by further influences which go far to explain why wartime fluctuations were so marked. These factors also affected the distribution of business by season. Of greatest effect was the adoption of a convoy system for merchant shipping. In the major wars fought by England with France and Spain in 1702-13, 1739-48, and 1756-63, and again in the lesser Anglo-Spanish wars of 1718-20 and 1727-9,[2] English vessels probably still made up the bulk of the vessels employed in the commerce.[3] But although some continued to sail alone, the menace of French and Spanish privateers drove most to sail with the warships provided by the Admiralty.[4] In general, warships were appointed for convoy duty at fairly short intervals: in the War of the Spanish Succession, for instance, probably at least every two or three months. But appreciable delays could occur before the escorts were made available and the merchant fleets actually sailed. In 1704 the merchant

[1] Ibid., 9 January 1741. Offley, Campion and Brooks' purchases of the upper Douro vintages of 1778-80, and the prices paid, also varied to some extent. Their purchases of red wines of the '78 vintage came to 3,125 pipes at an average price of 33·9 *milreis*: purchases of red wines in the next two vintages and their average prices, were respectively 3,663 pipes at 27·2 *milreis*, and 3,146 pipes at 28·5 *milreis*. O.F. (V.N.). Waste Book, 1779-85.

[2] Portugal was actively allied to England during the War of the Spanish Succession and from January 1762 in the Seven Years War; otherwise she remained neutral.

[3] See Chapter 6, pp. 89-90.

[4] On the general question of naval trade protection see J. H. Owen, *War at Sea under Queen Anne, 1702-1708* (Cambridge, 1938), *passim*, and two works by H. W. Richmond, *The Navy as an Instrument of Policy, 1558-1727* (Cambridge, 1953), *passim*, and *The Navy in the War of 1739-48* (Cambridge, 1920), 3 vols., *passim*.

vessels intended for Portugal in the autumn did not sail until the winter, for lack of adequate escorts,[1] while in 1707 the convoys appointed for June and August were about two months and six weeks late respectively in leaving English waters.[2] In late February 1708 the supply of English shipping as a whole was disrupted by the general embargo placed on merchant shipping.[3] The situation was not dissimilar in the later wars. During the War of the Austrian Succession occurred what may well have been the longest delay of all when the sailing of the merchant fleet and its escorts from England arranged for late 1739 was delayed for nearly a year.[4]

Inevitably the periodicity induced by the convoy system affected the distribution of trade between seasons and between years. The effect was most marked in the textile and wine trades. It was probably at its greatest when the outward-bound merchant fleet from England appointed for late 1739 was delayed for almost a year. In July 1740 the Envoy in Lisbon wrote that the English houses there had received no supplies from England for nine months, and that their warehouses were 'quite drained of all sorts of Goods particularly the Woolen'.[5] Two months earlier a wine shipper had written from Oporto that 'all lodges are full of wines and no ships to embark them in',[6] while in July the Oporto Consul observed 'this Factory is vastly uneasy at the delay of the Ships . . . from England, the Goods they have on Board being much wanted, as also the Vessells to carry home the Wines'.[7] By the end of August the ships had still not arrived and it was reported that the merchants at Oporto 'begin to despair of

[1] J. H. Owen, op. cit., p. 104.

[2] Ibid., pp. 207-9, 220-1.

[3] Ibid., p. 244. After 1708 the system of trade protection which had aroused much mercantile and Parliamentary criticism was appreciably improved, probably as a result of increased naval strength and the passing of the Convoys and Cruisers Act of that year, see ibid., pp. 69-70. The merchants in the trade with Portugal, however, continued to complain, as in August 1711 when the Oporto Factory spoke out against 'the uncertainty and neglect' of warships on convoy duty. They proposed that two convoys be appointed yearly for the ships bound for Oporto. Oporto Factory representation, 30 August 1711, P.R.O. C.O. 388/15, M.122. See also Lisbon Factory memorial, 1 October 1711, P.R.O. C.O. 388/15, M.123.

[4] H. W. Richmond, *The Navy in the War of 1739-48*, Vol. I, pp. 187-8. Although specific dates are not given, other evidence shows this happened in 1739-40.

[5] Tyrawly to Newcastle, 23 July 1740, P.R.O. S.P. 89/40.

[6] P.R.O. C.M.E. C.110 19, 20, Pratt *ex parte*. Hitchcock to Hitchcock, 7 May 1740.

[7] Parker to Newcastle, 18 July 1740, P.R.O. S.P. 89/41.

seeing them in the year 1740'.[1] The warships and their charges did not in fact reach Portugal until mid-October 1740, and apart from intermittent shipments in single ships, the accumulated wines did not leave Oporto until the end of November.

English grain shipments were, however, less affected by the convoy system because of the special disadvantages suffered under such a system. In the Lisbon Factory's view corn shipped from England 'very often by Lying long aboard, occasioned by the Delays and Uncertainties of Convoys, suffers very much and Great Part is damaged and perished before it Arrives'.[2] Moreover, sharp falls in grain prices could follow the arrival of numerous vessels: in Lisbon in August 1711, following the arrival of an English and then a Dutch fleet, corn prices fell by 'almost one half',[3] while in Oporto in May 1759 after the arrival of the 'fleet from England' with 10,000 sacks of wheat and the arrival, too, of 3,000 sacks from Lisbon, an English factor there thought they 'must . . . lower the Price greatly'.[4] Corn exporters were thus encouraged on occasion to forgo the safety of convoys and to charter ships to sail alone or 'on the run'.

The heightening of fluctuations in wartime also sprang from factors affecting the *amount* of trade carried on. For example, the stimulus given to the sale of English textiles by the boost Brazilian and Portuguese incomes received in the years of Anglo-French war, through the disturbance to the French colonial sugar trade, would have varied from year to year. Variations would have occurred too in the flow of English military supplies to Portugal in the War of the Spanish Succession.[5] The adverse effects of the campaigning in Portugal in this war and in 1762 must also have affected the flow of English exports.[6] The increase in freight rates that commonly occurred in wartime may also have discouraged business, especially

[1] P.R.O. C.M.E. C.110 19, 20, Pratt *ex parte*. Hitchcock to Hitchcock, 30 August 1740.

[2] Lisbon Factory memorial, 1 October 1711, P.R.O. C.O. 388/15, M.123. See also the petition of the London merchants trading to Portugal [September 1703], P.R.O. S.P. 89/88.

[3] Milner to Lewes, 26 August 1711, P.R.O. S.P. 89/21.

[4] H.R. (V.N.). Letter to W. Parsons, 26 May 1759, Letter Book, Dec. 1758-Oct. 1760.

[5] See Chapter 1, pp. 38-9.

[6] In 1762 'the distress brought upon [Portugal] by the March and Subsistence even of her own Troops, increase of Taxes and many other incidental circumstances' undoubtedly harmed British commerce, wrote the Envoy in Lisbon in 1769. Attachment to Lyttelton to Weymouth, f. 54, 21 June 1769, P.R.O. S.P. 89/69.

in the wine trade where freight charges were important. The normal peacetime rate for shipping a tun of wine from Oporto to England was 30s. But in January 1740 it had risen to 70s., in February 1741 to 90s., and in March and April 1741 to 100s.[1] Again, in May 1760 it had risen to 55s., and in November 1760 and May 1761 to 70s.[2] Such increases may well have inclined wine merchants to caution in their orders. They certainly did so in May 1740 in the case of Timothy Hutchinson, a Leeds wine merchant, who resolved 'to do very little in the wine trade this year, the wines being small and freight running high'.[3]

Finally, certain more miscellaneous events also disturbed the annual and seasonal flows of Anglo-Portuguese trade. They included the signing of the Methuen treaty in 1703, the devastation of Lisbon by earthquake in 1755, and the burning down of the Lisbon Custom House in 1764, all three events notably stimulating English exports to Portugal.[4] On the other hand, the occasions of substantial French illicit trade in Brazil would have had a contrary effect on English business, as in 1714 when the French 'spoil'd all Trade at [Rio de Janeiro] thirteen sail of their Ships having put in there under pretence of distress'.[5] Activity in the Portuguese wine trade was disturbed in the years immediately preceding 1756 by the acrimonious disputes between the English shippers and the Douro growers.[6] And the severe financial crises in England which punctuated the period as in 1710, 1720, 1726, 1745-6, 1761 and 1763, when merchants tended to reduce their trading commitments,[7] would have affected Anglo-Portuguese trade as a whole as they did other branches of English foreign trade.

[1] P.R.O. C.M.E. C.110 19, 20, Pratt *ex parte*. Hutchinson to Hitchcock, 7 January 1740. Hitchcock to Hitchcock, 4 February, 18 March, 1 April, 1741. In mid-1740, it will be recalled (see above, p. 118), general shipping prices from Oporto were about £26 a tun.

[2] H.R. (V.N.). Letter to G. Olive, 25 May 1760, Letter Book, Dec. 1758-Oct. 1760; letter to T. Lyde, 7 May 1761, Letter Book, Oct. 1760-Nov. 1765. Oporto Factory memorial, 30 April 1765, P.R.O. C.O. 388/53, Ll. 24, No. 27, Voucher C.

[3] P.R.O. C.M.E. C.110 19, 20, Pratt *ex parte*. Hutchinson to Hitchcock, 31 May 1740.

[4] See Chapter 1, pp. 38-9, and Chapter 2, p. 48.

[5] Brailsford to Brailsford, 5 November 1714, P.R.O. C.O. 388/17, N.237. Allegations were occasionally made too of English East Indiamen doing illicit business when calling in for refreshment at Brazilian ports.

[6] See Chapter 5, p. 78.

[7] T. S. Ashton, *Economic Fluctuations in England, 1700-1800*, Chapter V, *passim*.

FOREIGN TRADE AND THE ECONOMY

9 *The Portugal Trade and English Economic Development*

UNTIL RECENT YEARS wide agreement existed amongst historians on the major role of the expansion of English foreign trade in the seventeenth and eighteenth centuries in the causation of the English Industrial Revolution. In the last few years, however, the importance ascribed to trade has been somewhat diminished by the growing stress placed on other factors, among them demographic change, improving agricultural productivity, and the rise of more commercial and scientific attitudes. Nevertheless, many would still argue the great relevance of a preceding 'Commercial Revolution' for the Industrial Revolution, and it seems clear that commercial growth as a prime source of dynamism and change must still occupy a prominent position in any general attempt at explanation of the Industrial Revolution. Surprisingly little detailed examination has been made, however, of the actual relationships between trade growth and the general development of the economy, and this chapter attempts this for some of the relationships arising from Anglo-Portuguese trade. Attention will be focussed on the trade's significance for general commercial and financial development and for production.

In the first place, the trade had a considerable bearing on English commercial growth in the first sixty years of the eighteenth century, and especially so in the first forty years. In this discussion use can be made of the official English trade statistics. Their weaknesses are not unimportant but since the main changes in the commodities entering English trade, and their prices, did not occur until the closing decades of the century, the figures can be taken as broad approximations of the actual changes in English trade before 1760. Table 12 (a) shows the increase in the proportion of English exports that went to

Table XII ENGLISH EXPORTS AND PORTUGAL, 1700-1770

	(a) *Percentage of English Exports (excluding specie, including re-exports) shipped to Portugal*	(b) *Percentage of Exports of English Products and Manufactures shipped to Portugal*	(c) *Percentage of Exports of the principal Woollen Manufactures shipped to Portugal*
1700-4	8	12	11
1701-5	10	—	—
1706-10	10	13	12
1711-15	9	—	—
1716-20	10	14	15
1721-5	10	15	17
1726-30	11	—	—
1731-5	12	18	18
1736-40	12	18	20
1741-5	11	18	23
1746-50	10	14	17
1751-5	9	13	16
1756-60	10	14	18
1761-5	7	9	13
1766-70	4	6	9

Sources: (a). E. B. Schumpeter, *English Overseas Trade Statistics, 1697-1808*, Table I; C. Whitworth, *State of the Trade of Great Britain*, Part II, pp. 27-8. (b). Mrs E. B. Schumpeter's unpublished Radcliffe College Ph.D. thesis, 'Trade Statistics and Cycles in England 1697-1825' (1934), Table 2, with the missing figures for 1702-14 from T. S. Ashton, *Economic Fluctuations in England, 1700-1800*, Table 5, p. 184; P.R.O. Customs 3. (c). E. B. Schumpeter, *English Overseas Trade Statistics*, Table XII; P.R.O. Customs 3. The principal woollen goods shipped to Portugal include those in Appendix III, less wrought silk goods.

Portugal, with a peak of 12 per cent in the 1730s, while Table 12 (b) shows the same for exports of English products and manufactures, with a peak of 18 per cent in the 1730s and early 1740s. Total exports of English products and manufactures were growing only slowly in the first four decades of the century – from £4·75 million annually in 1706-10 they had risen to £6·09 million in 1736-40 – and this limited growth depended very much on increased shipments to Portugal, which rose from £0·62 million to £1·10 million annually between the two periods, an increase amounting to about one-third of the increase in total exports.[1]

[1] In the 1740s and 1750s the trade's importance for exports of English products and manufactures lessened, its increase between 1706-10 and 1756-60 amounting to about one-seventh of the increase in total exports.

Portugal was a very substantial market for English grainstuff exports. In the years 1721-7 and 1744-63 wheat shipments to Portugal amounted to 19 and 21 per cent respectively of total wheat exports averaging 149,000 and 348,000 quarters annually. In six of the years during these two periods wheat shipments to Portugal accounted for 30 per cent or more of total wheat exports, the peak year being 1760 when 46 per cent of the total 391,000 quarters exported went to Portugal.[1]

But Portugal's importance was greatest for exports of woollen and worsted goods, the most valuable group of English manufactured exports. The rise in the share of these exports going to Portugal can be seen in Table XII (c), the peak of 23 per cent being reached in 1741-5. Total shipments from England of the principal woollen manufactures grew only slightly in the early decades of the century – from £3·83 million annually in 1706-10 to £4·30 million in 1736-40 – and the increase in exports to Portugal, from £0·46 million annually to £0·86 million annually between these periods, amounted to about 85 per cent of the total increase.[2] The importance six of the leading woollen goods exported to Portugal had for their total trade is shown in Table XIII. In the case of bays, worsted stockings and hats, the increase in their shipment to Portugal between 1706-10 and 1736-40 amounted to about 85, 70 and 60 per cent respectively of the increase in their total exportation. In the 1760s the contraction in exports of English products and manufactures to Portugal undoubtedly contributed notably to the general contraction in shipments in that decade.[3]

Portugal's bearing on *recorded* imports into England was but moderate and had little effect on their growth: in none of the five-yearly periods between 1700 and 1770 did the annual value of imports from Portugal, as a proportion of total imports into England, rise

[1] Chol. (H.) MSS. P. 34/24: B.M. Add. MSS. 38,387, ff. 91 52: P.R.O. Customs 3. The other years were 1722 – 31 per cent, 1723 – 40 per cent, 1759 – 38 per cent, 1762 – 38 per cent, and 1763 – 32 per cent. It will be recalled, Chapter 1, p. 17n. that part of the grain declared for Portugal may have been actually unloaded in other countries, so that these figures may rather overstate the importance of Portugal.

[2] In the 1740s and 1750s Portugal's importance lessened, the increase in exports there between 1706-10 and 1756-60 amounting to about 30 per cent of the total increase.

[3] From an average of £10·28 million annually in 1761-5 total shipments slumped to £9·51 million annually in 1766-70. Average annual exports to Portugal fell from £0·94 million to £0·57 million respectively.

Table XIII ENGLISH WOOLLEN EXPORTS AND PORTUGAL, 1700-1770

	Short Cloths			*Long Cloths*		
	Total Exports	*Exports to Portugal*	*Percentage to Portugal*	*Total Exports*	*Exports to Portugal*	*Percentage to Portugal*
	(*£000 annual averages*)			(*£000 annual averages*)		
1706-10	153	34	22	470	24	5
1736-40	179	46	26	276	20	7
1756-60	552	155	28	520	100	19
1766-70	565	39	7	361	13	4
		Bays			*Worsted Stuffs*	
1706-10	426	159	37	563	52	9
1736-40	754	435	58	1,285	172	13
1756-60	1,176	443	38	1,859	167	9
1766-70	772	237	31	1,989	123	6
		Worsted Stockings			*Hats – Felt, Beaver and Castor*	
1706-10	84	30	36	44	14	33
1736-40	134	67	50	151	78	51
1756-60	238	80	34	200	89	45
1766-70	141	20	15	123	5	4

Sources: E. B. Schumpeter, *English Overseas Trade Statistics*, Table XII; P.R.O. Customs 3. Bays include double, minikin and single bays.

above 6 per cent. But if account is taken of the unrecorded imports of bullion, then imports from Portugal assume a greater importance. Between 1700 and 1760 the generally rising imports of bullion from Portugal into England, predominantly Portuguese gold coin, in settlement of the English current account surpluses, may in total have reached £25 million in value.[1] This sum would have amounted to about 6 per cent of all recorded imports into England in these decades. Such imports not only contributed notably to the growth of total imports into England, but meant that Portugal was the main source of gold entering England between 1700 and 1760.

English commercial growth was also furthered by Anglo-Portuguese trade in ways not indicated by the English trade statistics. In the period to 1770 Portugal was a growing market for North American cod consigned by West of England and colonial merchants, and in the 1760s, for colonial grainstuffs too. Her importance for American exports at the end of the period is shown in Table XIV.

[1] See Chapter 1, p. 20.

Table XIV THE TRADE BETWEEN ENGLISH NORTH AMERICA AND PORTUGAL, *c.* 1770

	Exports from the English Continental American Colonies (including Newfoundland) in 1770		*Average Annual Imports from English North America in 1772-3 into*	
	To the South of Europe	*Total Exports*	*Lisbon*	*Oporto*
Dried fish (quintals)	431,386	660,003 (£375,394)	64,257	44,398
Wheat (bushels)	588,561	851,240 (£131,467)	228,247	(£1,970)
Indian Corn (bushels)	175,221	578,349 (£43,376)	108,551	223
Bread and flour (£)	not available	504,553	79,801	—
Rice (£)	not available	340,693	8,931	8,482

Sources: D. MacPherson, *Annals of Commerce*, Vol. III, pp. 572-3; 'An Account of . . . all Goods . . . imported into . . . Portugal from Great Britain and her Colonies', P.R.O. B.T. 6/62.

The earnings of these trades for the most part were transferred to England,[1] the English balances, as a notable 'invisible' item, swelling English income from the main branches of the trade, while the American balances helped finance a higher level of exports from England to America than would otherwise have been possible. Both English 'invisible' earnings and the efficiency of the English Atlantic commercial system were promoted too by the opportunities given to the English and colonial-owned shipping engaged in the North American trades with Portugal to sail northwards to England or to Dutch and German ports laden with Portuguese wine and fruit.[2]

There were other English 'invisible' earnings associated with the Portugal trade. Most substantial were the earnings on the commercial credit extended to the Portuguese in the sale of English exports. Assuming an annual rate of interest of 5 per cent, and accepting the revised assessment of about 1758 that the annual indebtedness of the Portuguese in connection with English exports was about £1,500,000,[3] these earnings at the end of the 1750s would have been

[1] Chapter 4, pp. 71, 75-6. [2] Chapter 6, pp. 90-91. [3] See above, Chapter 3, pp. 59-60.

worth about £75,000 annually. Then the presence of large and wealthy English merchant communities in Portugal, coupled with the comparative financial weakness of the Portuguese, led to English participation in other branches of Portuguese commerce. Of the interests of the English merchants in Lisbon a contemporary wrote in 1730:

> comme ils sont puissans, ils ne bornent pas leur Commerce au seul trafic des Marchandises de leur Pais, ils y en sont venir de toutes les Parties de l'Europe . . . ils . . . employent quantité [de leurs vaisseaux] à porter pour eux . . . les Marchandises du crû de Portugal dans tous les endroits où elles sont convenables, principalement en Italie, comme à Gênes, à Ligourne, en Sicile, à Venise, &c. Enfin ils leur sont faire la même manoeuvre au retour.[1]

And some years later Lord Tyrawly wrote that when last in Lisbon, in 1752, he found that

> Our Merchants were become Universal Traders more than English Factors . . . many houses there dealt More or at least as Much in French Goods, Hamburg Linnen, Sicilian Corn, or other commodities from different countries than in the Produce of their own.[2]

Of the export trades, English interests were probably greatest in the re-export of sugar and other Brazilian products into the Mediterranean.[3] Of the import trades, that in corn probably attracted the greatest attention of houses in Portugal, as both principals and factors. One estimate of 1729 put corn imports into Portugal from 'Turkey' (the Levant) on 'English account' at about 150,000 *milreis* (£41,250) a year.[4] The interests in the corn trade probably grew much from the mid-1760s with the decline of English corn exports.

Then there were the freights earned by English shipping in Portuguese commerce. English vessels were employed in number in the trades with Madeira, the Azores and the Cape Verde islands. In 1773 nineteen English vessels entered Lisbon with cargoes from the

[1] *Description de la Ville de Lisbonne*, pp. 250-1.

[2] B.M. Add. MSS. 23,634, printed in A. R. Walford, *The British Factory in Lisbon*, p. 62.

[3] See above, Chapter 3, p. 61. On this business, see J. Cary, *An Essay towards Regulating the Trade of this Kingdom* (2nd edition, 1719), p. 85.

[4] Attachment to Compton to Newcastle, 6 August 1729 N.S., P.R.O. S.P. 89/35. On English interests in the Sicilian corn trade to Portugal and Spain see D. MacPherson, op. cit., Vol. III, p. 427.

islands, and in 1772 and 1773 fifteen and twenty-six laden vessels respectively cleared Lisbon for them.[1] English vessels were also engaged in the commerce with the North African settlement of Mazagão.[2] In the Brazil trades the use of English ships was permitted by the 1654 commercial treaty but how frequently they were employed is not clear. In 1722, when a ship owned by Browne and Company of Lisbon was hired to sail in the Rio de Janeiro fleet, it was stated that such business was 'almost annually practised'.[3] In Portuguese foreign trade their use was undoubtedly considerable. In 1729 an English merchant in Lisbon declared that the corn imported from the Levant and Italy was 'brought mostly in English bottoms':[4] and in 1765 the Lisbon Factory declared that 'Twenty Years ago . . . English Vessels . . . . were . . . in a great measure, the Carriers of all the Merchandize of the Mediterranean to this Port'.[5] This is further shown by figures of Lisbon's shipping movements at the period's end. In 1773, 36 English ships entered Lisbon with cargoes from foreign ports (excluding Britain, her colonies and Ireland), and in 1772 and 1773, 40 and 36 laden English vessels respectively cleared the capital for foreign ports.[6] Of the vessels clearing Lisbon in 1772, 7 were going 'to the North' and 33 'to the Mediterranean'. For 1773 the position was as shown in Table XV.

The English also had various financial interests in Portugal, probably on a more extensive scale than the evidence which has come to light suggests. They included foreign exchange dealing on behalf of the Portuguese Crown: in 1721 it was said that Ferdinand Wingfield, a leading Lisbon English merchant, had at different times 'supply'd the Court with bills for large Summs on Italy and Holland for the use of their Ministers'.[7] There was also a small but increasing volume

[1] Enclosures N.1 and 2, Walpole to Rochford, 4 July 1774, P.R.O. S.P. 89/77.

[2] *Description de la Ville de Lisbonne*, p. 251; B.M. Add. MSS. 11,569, f. 187.

[3] Lumley to Carteret, 31 May 1722 N.S., P.R.O. S.P. 89/30.

[4] Attachment to Compton to Newcastle, 6 August 1729 N.S., P.R.O. S.P. 89/35.

[5] Memorial of 24 July 1765, P.R.O. C.O. 388/95, f. 16. On this business see also *The British Merchant*, Vol. I, p. 3, and Burnett to Newcastle, 23 February 1726 N.S., B.M. Add. MSS. 11,570, f. 13.

[2] Enclosures N.1 and 2, Walpole to Rochford, 4 July 1774, P.R.O. S.P. 89/77. These figures exclude ships just calling or in ballast. In 1766 and 1772, 56 and 79 English ships respectively entered Lisbon with cargoes from foreign ports and the Portuguese Atlantic islands together. Ibid., and Attachment 2, Lyttelton to Weymouth, 13 March 1769, P.R.O. S.P. 89/67.

[7] Letter to Sir John Ward, 1 October 1721, P.R.O. S.P. 100/39.

Table XV ENGLISH VESSELS ENTERING AND CLEARING LISBON IN 1773

	Entering from	*Clearing to*
St. Petersburg	5	1
'Norway and the North'	—	5
Hamburg	—	10
Rotterdam	—	1
Ostend	—	3
Spanish ports	9	3
Mogadore	5	1
Genoa	8	11
Leghorn and Sicily	9	—
Rhodes	—	1
	36	36

of capital investment in Portugal, notably in the Douro wine industry. The earliest evidence dates from 1735 and concerns a vineyard, part of the estate of Birkhead Pratt, a deceased English merchant,[1] while in 1744 Bartholomew, Bearsley and Company owned some lodges for storing wines in the village of Salgueiral near Regoa.[2] In 1758 it was stated that 'the English have . . . Vineyards of their own bought in [the upper Douro]',[3] and in 1764 that they had erected 'houses and Stills in the Wine Country, purchasing some Lands'.[4] Capital was also invested in Portuguese shipping. In 1723 the English Consul in Lisbon referred to the English 'being frequently concerned in Portuguese ships':[5] in 1756 Holdsworth, Olive and Newman of Oporto had a half-share in one Portuguese vessel and in 1760 one-eighth and one-quarter shares in two others.[6] Money also went into the trading companies set up by Pombal, although in 1764 the Lisbon Envoy thought 'no considerable Sums' were involved and it was restricted to those who 'found their interest in obliging the Portuguese Ministers'.[7]

[1] P.R.O. C.M.E. C.110 19, 20, Pratt *ex parte*, Hitchcock to Hitchcock, 1 July 1735.

[2] Minute paper dated 2 January 1849 in the Vila Nova offices of Taylor, Fladgate and Yeatman. I am indebted to Mr Richard Yeatman for this information.

[3] Memorial of . . . the Merchants of Great Britain, 12 July 1758, P.R.O. S.P. 89/51.

[4] Memorial of . . . the Merchants of Great Britain, 31 October 1764, P.R.O. C.O. 388/53, Ll. 24, No. 20. See also Oporto Factory memorial, 30 April 1765, P.R.O. C.O. 388/53, Ll. 24, Nos. 20 and 26.

[5] B.M. Add. MSS. 11,569, f. 121.

[6] H.R. (V.N.). Journal, 1755-66; Ledger, 1759-65, f. 37.

[7] Hay to Halifax, 11 February 1764, P.R.O. S.P. 89/59. In 1760 the English Envoy in Lisbon reported that Mr Burry, the Lisbon correspondent of the London merchants

England's 'invisible' earnings at this time also benefited from the international business accruing to London in connection with the Dutch, German and other foreign merchants' trade balances in Portugal. The practice of remitting part of these balances initially to England in either bullion or bills of exchange[1] made London an important centre for the settlement of Portugal's trade accounts with northern Europe. The transmission of these balances by bill to the Continent gave business to exchange dealers, while those made in bullion promoted the business of bullion dealers. Alternatively, the sterling balances held in London by European merchants in consequence of their trade with Portugal may have been used to settle mutual trading debts, further promoting sterling as an international currency and London as an international payments centre. Note also needs to be taken, for the period from the late 1720s onwards, of the commissions earned in London from the entrepôt business conducted in Brazilian diamonds imported from Portugal.[2]

The great and persistent bullion inflow from Portugal on English account significantly aided English commerce by the support it gave to trade in times of temporary trade deficits or financial crises, and in particular by its sustaining of the branches of trade with chronic deficits, notably those with the Baltic region and the East Indies. Adam Smith described this function of the Portugal trade as 'facilitating all the different round-about trades of consumption which are carried on in Great Britain'.[3] Since the trade yielded only a little silver, its immediate aid to the settlement of the East India Company's trading deficits with Asia was slight. By substantially adding to

who then held the contract for the export of Portuguese diamonds, had subscribed to the Pernambuco Company 'probably to please the Conde d'Oeyras [Pombal]'. P.R.O. Chatham MSS. Vol. 94, f. 82. It is perhaps not surprising, given the hostility that the Wine Company of the Alto Douro aroused among the English, that only one English name – Diogo Archbald – figures among an early list of shareholders. J. de Macedo, *A Situação Económica no Tempo de Pombal*, p. 269.

[1] See above, Chapters 1, 2, and 7.

[2] For this business, see Chapter 1, p. 24.

[3] *The Wealth of Nations* (Cannan ed.), Vol. II, p. 51. Smith decried the great value contemporaries attached to the Portugal trade as the source of virtually all England's gold by pointing out that if England was entirely excluded from the trade she would still be able to obtain the gold she wanted for the purpose of plate or trade by purchasing it elsewhere like any other commodity. However, this neglects the point that without the large favourable balances of the Portugal trade over many years England's overall trade and payments balances would have been consistently smaller and hence too her ability to import bullion to facilitate the 'round-about' trades.

England's money stock, however,[1] the Portuguese gold helped keep down silver prices and enabled its export to continue. Its bearing on the Baltic deficits was more direct. There has been much discussion recently on how these were settled, by direct bullion shipments from England,[2] or through a multilateral payments system utilizing bills of exchange and Amsterdam.[3] The debate so far has proved inconclusive, except insofar as both methods seem to have been used. It is more than likely that Portuguese gold was important to both methods. Richard Cantillon writing in the mid-eighteenth century observed that the gold derived from the Portugal trade more than 'suffices . . . to pay the balance which England sends into Holland, Sweden, Muscovy and the other states where she is indebted'.[4] While the exchange dealings associated with the second method almost certainly had some bearing on the substantial bullion shipments from England to Holland during the general period under study,[5] in which shipments in the years following 1707 gold became increasingly important and predominantly so in the decade after 1717.[6]

Discussion of the significance of the Portugal trade for English production is hampered by the lack of satisfactory output statistics. The size of wheat shipments to Portugal though suggests they were of some importance to arable farmers in the corn exporting areas. But clearly the significance of the trade was greatest for the woollen and worsted industry. Miss Deane's rough estimates of its output between about 1695 and 1741 indicate that real output grew fairly markedly, perhaps by some 40 per cent, although in money terms the increase was less because of the fall in prices during the period.[7] It is

[1] This point is further discussed below.

[2] See C. Wilson: 'Treasure and Trade Balances: The Mercantilist Problem', *Ec.H.R.*, 2nd series, Vol. II (1949); 'Treasure and Trade Balances: Further Evidence', *Ec.H.R.*, 2nd series, Vol. IV (1951); 'International Payments: An Interim Comment', *Ec.H.R.*, 2nd series, Vol. XV (1962).

[3] See E. F. Heckscher, 'Multilateralism, Baltic Trade and the Mercantilists', *Ec.H.R.*, 2nd series, Vol. III (1950); J. M. Price, 'Multilateralism and/or Bilateralism: the Settlement of British Trade Balances with "The North", *c.* 1700', *Ec.H.R.*, Vol. XIV (1961); J. Sperling, 'The International Payments Mechanism in the Seventeenth and Eighteenth Centuries', *Ec.H.R.*, Vol. XIV (1962).

[4] R. Cantillon, *Essai sur la Nature du Commerce en Général* (ed. Higgs, 1931), p. 261, cited by C. Wilson, *Ec.H.R.* (1951), pp. 237-8.

[5] For recorded exports between 1698 and 1727 see J. M. Price, *Ec.H.R.* (1961), pp. 257-8.

[6] Ibid., pp. 256-7.

[7] P. Deane, 'The Output of the British Woollen Industry in the Eighteenth Century', *J.Ec.H.*, Vol. XVII (1957), pp. 207-23.

further suggested that at the end of the seventeenth century about two-fifths of the industry's output was exported.[1] If this export ratio is at all realistic for the early decades of the eighteenth century then the Portugal trade, whose increase was so important for the growth of English woollen exports between 1700 and 1740 must have substantially contributed to the growth of output. The impact of the trade on the constituent branches of the English woollen industry is also difficult to see. In the case of bays, however, it was clearly great. At the end of the seventeenth and the beginning of the eighteenth centuries Portugal was an important market for Essex bay-makers: in 1713 a number of Essex bay-making towns asserted that their exports went solely to Portugal.[2] After the War of the Spanish Succession a general decline occurred in bay-making in Essex,[3] and the expansion of Portuguese demands for bays may have slowed this process. It seems more likely, though, that the stimulus to bay-making chiefly applied to producers in the rising northern districts, especially the West Riding, contributing to the manufacture's establishment there by 1750.[4] The Portugal trade would also have stimulated output in the Norwich worsted stuff manufacture,[5] in the Midlands worsted stocking trades, and in the hat manufacture of London and Lancashire.

The trade also contributed to the improving organization of the domestic English economy at this time. It sustained a large and generally growing traffic of goods in England, in the raw materials of the textile industry as well as finished textiles, in grainstuffs, and in wines. Its needs also helped foster the improvements in London's mercantile and financial services. In the first half of the century the trade figured prominently among the London merchants' foreign

[1] Ibid., pp. 209-10.

[2] K. H. Burley, 'A Note on a Labour Dispute in Early Eighteenth-Century Colchester', *B.I.H.R.*, Vol. XXIX (1956), pp. 220-1, and D. A. E. Harkness, 'The Opposition to the 8th and 9th Articles of the Commercial Treaty of Utrecht', *Scottish Historical Review*, Vol. XXI (1924), p. 222.

[3] K. H. Burley, 'The Economic Development of Essex in the Later Seventeenth and Early Eighteenth Centuries' (unpublished University of London Ph.D. thesis, 1957), pp. 152-62.

[4] See K. H. Burley, *B.I.H.R.* (1956), pp. 220-30, and H. Heaton, *The Yorkshire Woollen and Worsted Industries* (Oxford, 1920), pp. 263-76.

[5] On the general prosperity of the Norwich stuff manufacture in the first half of the eighteenth century, see J. K. Edwards, 'The Economic Development of Norwich, 1750-1850' (unpublished University of Leeds Ph.D. thesis, 1963), Part I.

interests, and its growth must have stimulated the rise of specialist packers, shippers, warehousemen and exchange brokers. The nation-wide financial transactions associated with the trade would also have contributed to the evolution of a more efficient internal payments system.

There were also important implications for England's domestic currency and credit arrangements. Most of the increasing quantities of gold imported into England from Portugal probably went straight into circulation, either as Portuguese *moedas* or recoined into guineas. Between 1700 and 1760 gold imports from Portugal on English account approximately came to £25 million, while the circulation of gold in England grew, again approximately, from £9,500,000 in 1701, including foreign coin, to a circulation of guineas alone of £22,500,000 in 1773.[1] The trade was thus instrumental in a major way in the establishment of the gold standard in England in these years and in the displacement of silver.[2] By ensuring a growing stock of monetary metal the gold inflow also provided the basis for the Bank of England's expanding note issue and advances, as well as those of the London private banks. Contemporary opinion connected with the Portugal trade generally attached much importance to Portuguese gold for English currency and credit. In September 1759 a London Portugal merchant noting the delay in the Rio de Janeiro fleet's return to Lisbon thought the consequences 'may possibly prove to be a want of currency to circulate our paper',[3] and in 1766 the Envoy in Lisbon considered 'the publick Credit of [Great Britain] would be greatly affected by the want of the constant supplies of ready money which go from hence'.[4] One critic of these views, the anonymous author of *Occasional Thoughts on the Portuguese Trade*,[5] however, sought to refute those who supposed 'the Portuguese gold is absolutely necessary towards giving a currency to that paper money on which the credit of our Bank, merchants, and government seems to rely for support', by pointing out that some of the Portuguese

[1] J. Craig, *The Mint*, pp. 215, 245.

[2] On the turn to a gold standard, see A. Feavearyear, *The Pound Sterling*, 2nd edition (Oxford, 1963), Chapter VII.

[3] Grosett to Wood, 8 September 1759, P.R.O. S.P. 89/51.

[4] Hay to Conway, 1 March 1766, P.R.O. S.P. 89/62. See also Lisbon Factory memorial, 6 June 1760, P.R.O. C.O. 388/53, Ll. 20.

[5] Published in London in 1767.

coin circulating in England was the balance of English trade with European countries other than Portugal.[1] This is valid, but does not weaken the general point significantly. No doubt English banking and credit would have developed without the influx of Portuguese gold because of the other favourable forces making for such development; however, less conventional methods would have had to be adopted, including the greater use of paper securities, and probably growth would have been slower and even less stable than it was.

The trade also had some bearing on the course of English prices. Professor Ashton has stressed the importance of changes in the stock of monetary metals at this time as a partial explanation of price movements,[2] and it is very probable that the influx of Portuguese gold as a prime addition to English money supplies helped to slow the general tendency for prices to fall to the middle 'thirties, and to make them relatively more stable until about 1760. What effect the decline of Portuguese gold imports in the later 1760s had on English finance is not clear. Undoubtedly the quantity of *moedas* in circulation fell away sharply. In 1774 it was noted that since 'the profits of [the Portugal] trade have declined rapidly within these fifteen years . . . we see no more [Portuguese] gold in circulation'.[3] This development was made more serious by the radical fall in England's overall trade surplus which seems to have occurred simultaneously.[4] However, by the 1760s the English financial system had come a long way from its early eighteenth century form and was far better established, and, in particular, was less dependent on bullion as such through the increased use of paper securities.

There are a number of other financial themes which could be studied, and which would repay the further investigation that would be involved. In particular it would be interesting to examine the no doubt many uses to which the mercantile incomes made in the trade were put to, and also the contribution made by the trade to the formation of capital in England. One likely significant connection is

[1] Ibid., pp. 9 10, 38-9.

[2] *An Economic History of England: The 18th Century*, p. 198. See also Professor Habakkuk's comments on this in his review of Professor Ashton's book, *Ec.H.R.*, 2nd series, Vol. VIII (1956), pp. 436-7.

[3] Isaac de Pinto, *An Essay on Circulation and Credit*, p. 65 (translator's note.)

[4] C. Whitworth, *State of the Trade of Great Britain*, Part I, p. 79. The Bank of England's ratio of bullion and coin to notes in circulation and balances in drawing accounts was also significantly lower than usual in these years.

that between the merchants in the trade and the growth of financial dealings of different kinds, particularly in London. Unlike merchants in most branches of English trade, the Portugal merchants did not have to take their returns from abroad almost invariably in goods, but could take them in the easily negotiable form of bullion. Furthermore, as noted above, the Bank of England made loans to those who deposited gold with it. The Portugal merchants were thus well placed to combine trade with an interest in financial dealing, or to consider taking up the latter altogether. A glance at the available evidence suggests the connection may have been impressive. As mentioned earlier, three of the five known Portugal merchants selling gold to the Bank of England in 1711-12, John Ward, Sir John Houblon and Peter Delmé, were simultaneously directors of the Bank;[1] Sir Henry Furnese, the financial contractor in the War of the Spanish Succession, also had interests, probably commercial, in the Portugal trade;[2] while William Braund offers the interesting case of a merchant who evolved from being an exporter of woollens to Lisbon into a bullion importer and finally an insurance dealer between 1741 and 1763.[3] Of other likely fields of interest private banking may well have been prominent, and it would be interesting to examine the new formations in the period with this connection in mind.[4]

Thus between 1700 and 1770 Anglo-Portuguese trade contributed in a number of not unimportant ways to the development of the English economy, and especially so in the first forty years of the century when the rate of overall development was not particularly impressive. Without the growth of this trade, without the expansion of Brazilian gold output on which so much else turned, English commercial, financial and industrial advance would have been even slower. Here we have been concerned with only one branch of English trade. But if its stimulus to economic advance is viewed in combination with that exerted by the other branches with expansive tendencies, then evidently the impact of foreign trade on the economy at large was substantial. This study of the Portugal trade supports the

[1] See above, Chapter 7, pp. 104-5. Sir John Houblon was the first Governor of the Bank.

[2] See his undated representation, P.R.O. S.P. 89/89.

[3] L. S. Sutherland, *A London Merchant*, p. 16.

[4] For the predominantly mercantile and manufacturing origins of the new formations, see D. M. Joslin, 'London Private Bankers, 1720-1785', *Ec.H.R.*, 2nd series, Vol. VII (1954), pp. 180-1.

view that whilst the growth of foreign trade may not have directly precipitated the Industrial Revolution, its contribution was nevertheless notable, in the way in which it helped prepare the economy for 'take-off', and in particular by sustaining the progress of commercial and financial activities.

Note on the use of the official English trade statistics

THE TRADE FIGURES compiled annually by the Inspectors-General of the Customs, P.R.O. Customs 3, best measure changes in the volume rather than the value of transactions in eighteenth-century trade.[1] But there are grounds for thinking that they do offer some guide to long-term movements in the value of the trade between England and Portugal in the first three-quarters of the century. It is true that the official valuations of exports remained virtually unchanged after 1715 or so. And that the prices of the chief exports, woollen and worsted textiles, so far as we are aware with the limited evidence available, tended to fall between about 1715 and the mid-century, the fall being reversed either before or during the Seven Years War. Because of this the official figures probably over-estimate the actual value of exports to Portugal between about 1715 and 1750 and under-estimate it afterwards. Import valuations too remained virtually unchanged, but the prices of wines, the chief recorded import from Portugal, were generally stable over the period, so that import values are broadly realistic. There are, of course, other sources of error: the tendency to overstatement of their shipments by exporters, the exclusion of freight and insurance payments on imports, and the smuggling that went on – undoubtedly Portuguese wines were illegally run into England although the French wines coming from the Channel Islands and elsewhere as Portuguese probably more than compensated this. These points suggest that the official statistics further tend rather to exaggerate actual export values and to understate actual import values. Nevertheless with these reservations in mind, the official figures do offer an approximate guide to movements in the trade.

[1] On the use of the Inspectors-General figures see G. N. Clark, *Guide to English Commercial Statistics, 1696-1782* (1938), pp. 33-42, and the introduction by T. S. Ashton to E. B. Schumpeter, *English Overseas Trade Statistics, 1697-1808* (Oxford, 1960), pp. 1-9.

List of Appendixes

THE TRADE BETWEEN ENGLAND AND PORTUGAL, 1697-1773
(£000)

	Exports to Portugal	*Imports from Portugal*	*Export Surplus*
1697	125	87	39
1698	365	155	210
1699	338	165	173
1700	336	279	57
1701	277	207	70
1702	460	194	266
1703	714	257	457
1704	781	331	450
1705	819	223	596
1706	763	242	521
1707	615	241	374
1708	538	272	267
1709	732	252	479
1710	615	192	423
1711	576	247	329
1712	565	202	362
1713	628[1]	196	432
1714	794	281	512
1715	625	333	292
1716	753	303	449
1717	618	339	279
1718	514	429	85
1719	816	356	460
1720	776	319	456
1721	771	423	349
1722	973	364	610
1723	865	350	515
1724	667	389	278
1725	781	411	370
1726	866	231	634
1727	793	400	393
1728	899	496	403
1729	996	442	555
1730	1,016	228	788
1731	903	364	539
1732	1,022	295	727
1733	1,142	300	842
1734	1,007	311	696
1735	1,046	358	687
1736	1,262	304	958
1737	1,349	387	962
1738	1,405	306	1,099

1 This figure was incorrectly printed by Whitworth as £528,000.

	Exports to Portugal	*Imports from Portugal*	*Export Surplus*
1739	1,018	305	713
1740	789	202	587
1741	1,321	554	768
1742	1,154	492	662
1743	1,145	466	679
1744	889	212	677
1745	1,065	418	647
1746	1,052	306	746
1747	1,239	360	879
1748	1,082	321	760
1749	990	388	602
1750	1,208	244	964
1751	1,158	259	899
1752	939	253	686
1753	1,156	332	824
1754	1,165	254	911
1755	1,073	263	810
1756	1,513	172	1,341
1757	1,588	282	1,306
1758	889	257	632
1759	1,222	273	949
1760	1,292	299	992
1761	1,264	242	1,022
1762	909	359	550
1763	728	304	424
1764	1,244	313	931
1765	679	354	325
1766	667	348	319
1767	515	340	175
1768	712	392	320
1769	545	369	176
1770	535	330	205
1771	716	355	361
1772	635	347	288
1773	522	349	173

Source: C. Whitworth, *State of the Trade of Great Britain*, Part II, pp. 27-8. (The totals were drawn from the Ledgers of the Inspectors-General, P.R.O. Customs 3.)

RE-EXPORTS OF FOREIGN AND COLONIAL GOODS FROM ENGLAND TO PORTUGAL, 1700-1770
(ANNUAL AVERAGES, £000)

1700-4	25
1706-10	29
1711-15	—
1716-20	36
1721-5	37
1726-30	—
1731-5	41
1736-40	52
1741-5	34
1746-50	22
1751-5	—
1756-60	22
1761-5	20
1766-70	—

Source: P.R.O. Customs 3.

APPENDIX III

THE PRINCIPAL ENGLISH TEXTILES EXPORTED TO PORTUGAL, 1700-1770
(ANNUAL AVERAGES)

	Value (£000)	*Value of the Principal Textiles Exported as a Percentage of Total English Exports to Portugal*
1700-4	358	70
1701-5	430	71
1706-10	463	71
1711-15	488	77
1716-20	555	80
1721-5	620	76
1726-30	729	80
1731-5	744	73
1736-40	871	75
1741-5	882	79
1746-50	848	76
1751-5	799	73
1756-60	1,086	84
1761-5	709	74
1766-70	459	77

The products comprise short, long and Spanish cloths, single, double and minikin bays, perpetuanas and serges, worsted stuffs, woollen and worsted stockings, hats of felt, beaver and castor, wrought silk, and cottons. Their export values are from P.R.O. Customs 3, total export values used are those in C. Whitworth, op. cit., Part II, pp. 27-8, with export values in 1713 corrected to £628,000.

The value of the principal textile exports for the years 1705, 1712 and 1727, for which the Inspectors-General ledgers are missing, were estimated in the following manner. The aggregated textile exports for the years 1698-1734 for which figures were available were closely correlated ($r = \cdot 95$) with the figures of total exports given in C. Whitworth, op. cit. A linear relationship was therefore obtained by the method of least squares relating textile exports to total exports. The known values of total exports were then used to estimate the missing values of textile exports.

APPENDIX IV

WHEAT SHIPMENTS FROM ENGLAND TO PORTUGAL, 1700-1770 (ANNUAL AVERAGES)

	Quarters (000)	*Value* (£000)	*Value of Wheat Shipments as a Percentage of Total English Exports to Portugal*
1700-4	41	56	11
1706-10	59	80	12
1711-15	—	—	—
1716-20	7	9	1
1721-5	39	53	7
1726-30	—	—	—
1731-5	92	124	12
1736-40	84	114	10
1741-5	44	59	5
1746-50	68	92	8
1751-5	65	88	8
1756-60	53	71	6
1761-5	90	121	13
1766-70	5	7	1

Sources: Wheat figures from P.R.O. Customs 3, and total exports from C. Whitworth, op. cit., Part II, pp. 27-8.

WINES IMPORTED INTO ENGLAND FROM PORTUGAL, 1698-1770
(ANNUAL AVERAGES)

	Tuns (000)	*Value (£000)*	*Value of Wine Imports as a Percentage of Total Imports from Portugal*
1698-1702	6·6	142	71
1700-4	7·8	176	69
1701-5	8·0	173	71
1706-10	8·0	170	71
1711-15	7·7	217	86
1716-20	11·2	288	83
1721-5	13·1	326	84
1726-30	11·9	302	84
1731-5	11·5	287	88
1736-40	10·5	263	87
1741-5	13·1	367	86
1746-50	11·0	275	85
1751-5	9·2	230	85
1756-60	8·8	220	86
1761-5	10·5	257	82
1766-70	11·7	293	82

Sources: The tunnage and value figures are from P.R.O. Customs 3, total import values are from C. Whitworth, op. cit., Part II, pp. 27-8.

The tunnage and value of wine imports for the years 1705, 1712 and 1727 for which the Inspectors-General ledgers are missing were estimated in the following manner. The aggregated wine imports, tunnage and value, for the years 1698-1734 for which figures were available were closely correlated ($r = \cdot 998$ and ·97 respectively) with the tunnage figures of wine imports from Portugal into Great Britain in Appendix N of J. Warre, *The Past, Present and Future State of the Wine Trade*, p. 99, and with the value figures of total imports from Portugal printed in C. Whitworth, op. cit., respectively. Linear relationships were therefore obtained by the method of least squares relating the first to the second series in each case. The known values of the two second series were then used to estimate the missing values in the two first series.

LONDON RATE OF EXCHANGE ON LISBON, 1700-1770
(SHILLINGS AND PENCE PER MILREIS)

	First January Quotation	Annual Average of First Rate Quoted Each Month		First January Quotation	Annual Average of First Rate Quoted Each Month
1700	6s. 2d.	6s. 1d.	1736	5s. 6d.	5s. 5⅞d.
1701	6s. 0½d.	5s. 10⅛d.	1737	5s. 5½d.	5s. 5¾d.
1702	5s. 9¾d.	5s. 9⅝d.	1738	5s. 5½d.	5s. 5½d.
1703	5s. 8⅞d.	5s. 9⅞d.	1739	5s. 5⅝d.	5s. 5¼d.
1704	6s. 0½d.	6s. 0⅝d.			
1705	5s. 10¾d.	5s. 9⅝d.	1740	5s. 5d.	5s. 4⅞d.
1706	5s. 10½d.	5s. 9⅝d.	1741	5s. 4⅞d.	5s. 5¼d.
1707	5s. 9½d.	5s. 7½d.	1742	5s. 5¼d.	5s. 5½d.
1708	5s. 3⅝d.	5s. 2¼d.	1743	5s. 5⅝d.	5s. 6⅛d.
1709	5s. 5d.	5s. 5d.	1744	5s. 6d.	5s. 5d.
			1745	5s. 4⅝d.	5s. 4⅝d.
1710	5s. 7d.	5s. 6¼d.	1746	5s. 2¼d.	5s. 4¼d.
1711	5s. 1½d.	5s. 1½d.	1747	5s. 4¾d.	5s. 5⅛d.
1712	5s. 0¼d.	5s. 3d.	1748	5s. 4¼d.	5s. 4¾d.
1713	5s. 3d.	5s. 3⅝d.	1749	5s. 5⅜d.	5s. 5½d.
1714	5s. 4¾d.	5s. 5¼d.			
1715	5s. 5¾d.	5s. 5⅛d.	1750	5s. 6¼d.	5s. 5¾d.
1716	5s. 5½d.	5s. 5⅞d.	1751	5s. 5¾d.	5s. 5⅝d.
1717	5s. 6¾d.	5s. 6½d.	1752	5s. 5¾d.	5s. 6d.
1718	5s. 5¾d.	5s. 5½d.	1753	5s. 6⅛d.	5s. 6⅛d.
1719	5s. 4¾d.	5s. 4⅜d.	1754	5s. 5¾d.	5s. 5¾d.
			1755	5s. 5⅝d.	5s. 5d.
1720	5s. 5d.	5s. 3⅞d.	1756	5s. 4¼d.	5s. 4¾d.
1721	5s. 2½d.	5s. 4¼d.	1757	5s. 4⅞d.	5s. 4⅝d.
1722	5s. 2¼d.	5s. 4¼d.	1758	5s. 4½d.	5s. 5⅜d.
1723	5s. 4½d.	5s. 5d.	1759	5s. 5½d.	5s. 5⅝d.
1724	5s. 4⅜d.	5s. 5⅜d.			
1725	5s. 5¾d.	5s. 5⅝d.	1760	5s. 5⅜d.	5s. 5⅞d.
1726	5s. 5⅛d.	5s. 4⅜d.	1761	5s. 5¼d.	5s. 5¾d.
1727	5s. 4¾d.	5s. 5⅛d.	1762	5s. 5d.	5s. 6⅛d.
1728	5s. 5¼d.	5s. 6d.	1763	5s. 6d.	5s. 6⅝d.
1729	5s. 5⅞d.	5s. 6⅛d.	1764	5s. 5¼d.	5s. 5½d.
			1765	5s. 5⅝d.	5s. 5⅞d.
1730	5s. 6½d.	5s. 6¼d.	1766	5s. 6d.	5s. 6½d.
1731	5s. 5⅝d.	5s. 5⅝d.	1767	5s. 6¼d.	5s. 6¾d.
1732	5s. 5¾d.	5s. 5¾d.	1768	5s. 6¾d.	5s. 6⅝d.
1733	5s. 5⅝d.	5s. 5½d.	1769	5s. 6⅜d.	5s. 7d.
1734	5s. 4⅞d.	5s. 5⅛d.			
1735	5s. 5⅞d.	5s. 6d.	1770	5s. 6⅝d.	5s. 6⅞d.

Source: J. Castaing, *Course of the Exchange.*

GOLD PRICES AT LONDON, 1719-1770
(£ PER OUNCE IN BARS)

	Annual Average of First Price Quoted Each Month				*Annual Average of First Price Quoted Each Month*		
	£	s.	d.		£	s.	d.
1719	3	18	$0\frac{1}{8}$	1746	3	17	11
1720	3	19	0	1747	3	18	$4\frac{1}{8}$
1721	3	18	$2\frac{7}{8}$	1748	3	18	$1\frac{3}{4}$
1722	3	17	$11\frac{1}{8}$	1749	3	17	$10\frac{1}{2}$
1723	3	18	$1\frac{1}{4}$				
1724	3	17	$11\frac{1}{4}$	1750	3	17	$11\frac{7}{8}$
1725	3	17	11	1751	3	17	$10\frac{7}{8}$
1726	3	17	$10\frac{1}{8}$	1752	3	18	$0\frac{1}{4}$
1727	3	17	10	1753	3	18	4
1728	3	18	$4\frac{7}{8}$	1754	3	18	0
1729	3	18	$9\frac{3}{8}$	1755	3	17	$10\frac{3}{4}$
				1756	3	17	$10\frac{3}{4}$
1730	3	18	$7\frac{3}{8}$	1757	3	17	$11\frac{1}{8}$
1731	3	18	$0\frac{3}{4}$	1758	3	18	$8\frac{3}{8}$
1732	3	18	$0\frac{3}{4}$	1759	3	19	$4\frac{3}{8}$
1733	3	18	$2\frac{1}{8}$				
1734	3	18	$1\frac{1}{8}$	1760	3	18	$9\frac{3}{8}$
1735	3	18	$4\frac{3}{8}$	1761	3	19	$9\frac{1}{4}$
1736	3	18	$1\frac{1}{2}$	1762	3	19	$2\frac{3}{4}$
1737	3	18	$1\frac{3}{8}$	1763	4	0	$1\frac{5}{8}$
1738	3	18	$0\frac{5}{8}$	1764	3	18	$1\frac{3}{4}$
1739	3	17	$11\frac{3}{8}$	1765	3	18	$1\frac{3}{8}$
				1766	3	19	$0\frac{3}{8}$
1740	3	17	$11\frac{1}{8}$	1767	3	19	$6\frac{1}{4}$
1741	3	18	$3\frac{1}{2}$	1768	3	19	$2\frac{7}{8}$
1742	3	18	$4\frac{7}{8}$	1769	4	0	$2\frac{3}{8}$
1743	3	18	$9\frac{7}{8}$				
1744	3	18	$11\frac{5}{8}$	1770	4	0	$1\frac{1}{4}$
1745	3	18	$8\frac{5}{8}$				

Source: J. Castaing, *Course of the Exchange.*

HOME PORTS OF NEWFOUNDLAND COD SHIPS UNLOADING IN OPORTO, 1767-1770

	1767-8	*1768-9*	*1769-70*	*Total*
Dartmouth	7	8	6	21
Poole	4	4	9	17
Exeter/Topsham	3	4	4	11
Teignmouth	4	2	2	8
London	2	1	0	3
Liverpool	1	2	0	3
Weymouth	0	1	1	2
Portsmouth	1	0	0	1
Ross	1	0	0	1
Bristol	0	0	1	1
Halifax (Nova Scotia)	1	2	0	3
Placentia (Newfoundland)	0	1	0	1
Quebec	0	1	0	1
	24	27[1]	23	74

[1] The details of one ship are lacking for this season.

Source: H.R. (V.N.). Rough Book, 1766-9.

APPENDIX IX

OPORTO'S NEWFOUNDLAND COD AGENCY BUSINESS, 1767-1770

	1767-8		*1768-9*		*1769-70*	
Agents	*Ships*	*Quintals*	*Ships*	*Quintals*	*Ships*	*Quintals*
Holdsworth, Olive and Newman	16	27,433	17	27,705	15	27,049
Stafford & Co.	6	12,715	6	12,200	6	13,350
Bearsley & Webb	1	1,750	—	—	—	—
Clies & Co.	1	3,000	—	—	—	—
Clies & Babbington	—	—	2	4,000	—	—
Vincent & Co.		—	1	1,874	—	—
Lambert & Co.	—	—	1	1,000	—	—
T. Croft & Co.	—	—	—	—	2	4,700
	24	44,898	27	46,779	23	45,099

Source: H.R. (V.N.). Rough Book, 1766-9.

VESSELS CLEARING ENGLISH PORTS FOR PORTUGAL, 1715-1717

	Clearing from London			Clearing from the Outports			Total Clearances from England	
	Number	Total tonnage	Average tonnage	Number	Total tonnage	Average tonnage	Number	Average tonnage
1715	101	8,629	85	125	8,161	65	226	74
1716	134	11,766	88	124	8,318	67	258	78
1717	102	8,152	80	103	6,451	63	205	71

Sources: P.R.O. C.O. 390/8B; C.O. 390/5, Part I, f. 71.

APPENDIX XI

VESSELS CLEARING BRITISH PORTS FOR PORTUGAL AND MADEIRA, 1771-1775

	British-owned			Foreign-owned			Total Clearances	Average tonnage
	Number	Tons	Average tonnage	Number	Tons	Average tonnage		
1771	141	15,561	110	16	1,954	122	157	112
1772	156	18,029	116	11	1,898	173	167	119
1773	124	14,735	119	11	1,325	120	135	119
1774	158	19,357	123	12	1,930	161	170	125
1775	168	18,620	111	10	956	96	178	110

Source: P.R.O. B.T. 6/185.

APPENDIX XII

VESSELS ENTERING BRITISH PORTS FROM PORTUGAL AND MADEIRA, 1771-1775

	British-owned			Foreign-owned			Total Entries	Average tonnage
	Number	Tons	Average tonnage	Number	Tons	Average tonnage		
1771	257	25,758	100	11	968	88	268	100
1772	280	25,214	90	6	480	80	286	90
1773	297	27,798	94	6	1,180	197	303	96
1774	299	28,686	96	7	630	90	306	96
1775	286	28,175	99	5	650	130	291	99

Source: P.R.O. B.T. 6/185.

VESSELS CLEARING FROM THE ENGLISH OUTPORTS FOR PORTUGAL, 1715-1717

	1715	*1716*	*1717*	*Total*
Whitehaven	0	1	1	2
Lancaster	2	2	1	5
Poulton	0	0	1	1
Liverpool	4	5	4	13
Chester	4	5	5	14
Beaumaris	0	0	1	1
Llanelly	0	1	1	2
Milford	2	1	2	5
Swansea	2	2	0	4
Bristol	9	9	7	25
Bridgwater	0	2	2	4
Ilfracombe	0	0	1	1
Bideford	3	0	1	4
Padstow	1	0	1	2
St Ives	2	0	0	2
Penzance	3	3	0	6
Penryn	2	2	0	4
Gweek	0	3	1	4
Falmouth	6	7	7	20
Fowey	5	2	4	11
Looe	0	1	0	1
Plymouth	5	1	2	8
Dartmouth	1	0	2	3
Exeter	19	18	18	55
Lyme	0	0	2	2
Weymouth	1	0	0	1
Poole	1	1	0	2
Cowes	2	2	1	5
Southampton	10	6	5	21
Portsmouth	8	3	2	13
Dover	2	3	1	6
Sandwich	7	1	2	10
Yarmouth	1	7	3	11
Kings Lynn	7	7	6	20
Boston	0	1	1	2
Hull	5	8	5	18
Bridlington	0	1	0	1
Whitby	3	3	1	7
Stockton	2	0	0	2
Newcastle	5	14	12	31
Berwick	1	2	0	3
Total	125	124	103	352

Source: P.R.O. C.O. 390/8B.

DECLARED DESTINATIONS OF VESSELS CLEARING ENGLISH PORTS FOR PORTUGAL, 1715-1717

	Clearing from London			*Clearing from the Outports*			
	1715	*1716*	*1717*	*1715*	*1716*	*1717*	*Total*
Lisbon	45	53	33	68	53	44	296
Oporto	18	25	23	36	53	48	203
Figueira	3	5	4	10	2	2	26
Viana	1	0	2	3	9	7	22
Aveiro	0	0	0	3	5	1	9
Faro	1	0	0	3	2	1	7
Portugal	33	51	40	2	0	0	126
Total	101	134	102	125	124	103	689

Sources: P.R.O. C.O. 390/8B; C.O. 390/5, Part I, f. 71.

APPENDIX XV

PORTS OF ORIGIN OF VESSELS ENTERING LONDON FROM PORTUGAL, 1717-1719

	1717	*1718*	*1719*	*Total*
Lisbon	53	61	74	188
Oporto	74	105	80	259
Figueira	18	20	17	55
Viana	6	8	4	18
Faro	3	7	6	16
Vila Nova	1	1	2	4
Aveiro	0	0	1	1
Total	155	202	184	541

Source: P.R.O. C.O. 390/5, Part I, ff. 71, 72, 76.

List of Sources and Works Consulted

Manuscript Sources

IN ENGLAND

Public Record Office

Colonial Office

Board of Trade (Commercial)

Original Correspondence	C.O. 388. Vols 1-95.
Entry Books	C.O. 389. Vols 11-59.
Miscellanea	C.O. 390. Vols 5-9, 12-14.

Board of Customs and Excise

Ledgers of Imports and Exports	Customs 3, 1697-1775.

Board of Trade

Miscellanea	B.T.6. Various volumes.

State Paper Office

Portugal	S.P.89. Vols 15-92.
Foreign Ministers in England	S.P.100. Vols 37-43.

Chancery. Judicial Proceedings

Chancery Masters' Exhibits

C.107 171. Rebello v. Barons.

C.108 414. Unknown cause (re M. Kendrick of London).

C.109 348. Rucker v. Taylor.

C.110 19, 20. Pratt *ex parte*.

Chatham Papers

P.R.O. 30/8. Vol. 94.

British Museum

Egerton MSS. 528-9; 891; 921; 2,395; 2,423; 2,529.

Harley MSS. 2262-3.

Sloane MSS. 505; 2294; 2902.
Stowe MSS. 324-5.
Additional MSS. 8133B,C; 9,744; 11,569-70; 15,181; 19,034; 20,804; 20,847; 20,957-8; 21,438; 21,491; 22,857; 22,908; 23,627-42; 23,644-5; 23,726; 27,344; 28,056-7; 28,079; 29,590; 30,003; 32,788; 32,804; 32,807-8; 32,833; 32,860; 32,888; 33,038-9; 33,053; 33,125; 34,333; 34,335; 34,419-20; 34,744; 35,100-01; 35,839; 36,785; 38,332; 38,339; 38,424; 38,510; 40,015; 40,758; 40,760.

Bank of England
General Ledgers, I-VIII.

Corporation of London Record Office: The Guildhall
MSS. 6645/3/4/5.
9062/46.

University Library, Cambridge
Cholmondeley (Houghton) MSS. P. 26, 127/1-127/3; P. 28, 13/1-13/7; P. 28, 26; P. 34, 22; P. 34, 24; P. 34, 37/1-37/2; P. 41, 18/1-18/9; P. 41, 29; P. 41, 30/1-30/2; P. 41, 53; P. 43, 9; P. 44, 4; P. 44, 29; P. 44, 50; P. 54, 10; P. 63, 72; P. 63, 91; P. 89, 17/1-17/2; P. 89, 51/1-51/2; P. 91, 12; P. 91, 42; P. 91, 158.

Offley, Forrester and Company, London
Robert Wilmot's Ledger, 1708-1714.

IN PORTUGAL

Arquivo Torre de Tombo, Lisbon

Arquivo dos Feitos Findos	Conservatoria Inglesa, Maço VI, VII.
Junta do Comercio	Livro de Registo, 90.
Ministerio dos Negocios Estrangeiros	Maço IV, VI, VII.

Biblioteca Nacional, Lisbon

Colecção Pombalina	Cod. 42, 93-4, 122, 255, 458, 460, 495, 610-11, 613-14, 616, 625, 635-9, 646, 650-1, 653, 656-7, 687, 691-2, 694, 738,
Fundo Geral	231, 427, 441, 607, 1448, 2276, 10714.
	Caixa 5 B-7-12. 'Noticias de Portugal Sec. XVIII.'
	Caixa 72, 76.

Gabinete de Historia do Porto
Próprias da Câmara Municipal, Livro 50.
Registo Geral da Camara Municipal, Livro 7.

Real Companhia dos Vinhos do Porto
Various business records of the 1760s.

Hunt, Roope and Company, Vila Nova de Gaia
Business records dating from 1755, including Journals, Account and Sale Books, Letter Books, etc.

Offley, Forrester and Company, Vila Nova de Gaia
Journals and Waste Books, 1779-1785.

Contemporary Printed Sources

COLLECTIONS

Calendar of House of Lords MSS: New Series, 1693-5 – 1712-14.
Calendar of State Papers, Colonial Series. America and West Indies: 1700 – 1735-6.
Calendar of Treasury Papers: 1697-1728.
Calendar of Treasury Books: 1695-1718.
Calendar of Treasury Books and Papers: 1729-1745.
Journal of the Commissioners for Trade and Plantations: 1704-1782.

PAMPHLETS AND BOOKS

Place of publication London, unless otherwise stated.

ANONYMOUS, *An Account of the Court of Portugal* (1700).

A Full . . . Account of the Late Conspiracy in Portugal (1759).

The Advantages and Disadvantages which will attend the Prohibition of the Merchandises of Spain. A Sussex Farmer (1740).

Arte e Diccionario do Commercio e Economía Portugueza (Lisbon, 1784).

The Eighth and Ninth Articles of the Treaty of Commerce, with relation to the Trade of Scotland with France, Considered (1713).

The Case of the British Merchants Trading to Portugal [?1690].

Cautions to those who are to Chuse Members to serve in Parliament (1713).

A Collection of Petitions presented to the Honourable House of Commons against the Trade with France (1713).

Considerations on the Trade to Newfoundland [?c. 1710].

Description do la Ville do Lisbonne (Paris, 1730).

État Présent du Royaume de Portugal en L'Année MDCCLXVI (Lausanne, 1775).

ANONYMOUS, *A Letter to the Merchants of the Portugal Committee from a Lisbon Trader*. Publicus. (1754).

Letters from Barbary, France, Spain, Portugal, &c (1788).

Letters from Portugal on the Late and Present State of that Kingdom (1777).

Memorials of the British Consul and Factory at Lisbon (1766).

Mercator's Letters on Portugal and its Commerce (1754).

The National Merchant: or Discourse on Commerce and Colonies (1736).

Money of England reduced into Money of Portugal (Falmouth, 1766).

Os Privilegios do Inglez nos Reynos e Dominios de Portugal (1736).

Reasons for the Present Application to Parliament for Liberty to Import Salt from any Part of Europe directly into His Majesty's Colonies in America [1750].

Reasons humbly offer'd against opening a Trade with France for Wines [?1713].

Reasons humbly offer'd by the Merchants Trading to Spain and Portugal against the Bill for Suspending the Duty . . . on French Wines [1713].

Reasons humbly offered by the Merchants trading in Wine for Encouraging the better Carrying on the Said Trade [?1720].

Reasons humbly offer'd by the Portugal, Italian, and Spanish Merchants against Importing French Wines, in Returns for Tobacco (1709).

Occasional Thoughts on the Portuguese Trade (1767).

Whereas the Portugal Trade is very advantageous . . . [?1695].

Several Years Travels through Portugal, Spain . . . and the United Provinces (1702).

A Trip to Portugal, or a View of their Strength by Sea and Land (1704).

A General View of England Respecting its Policy, Trade, Commerce, Taxes . . . Argumentatively Stated from the Year 1600 to 1762. By M.V.D.M., trans. from the French. (1766).

ANDERSON, A. *An Historical and Chronological Deduction of the Origin of Commerce*, 2 vols (1764).

ANSON, G. *A Voyage Round the World in the Years 1740-1744*, 2nd ed. (1748).

BARETTI, G. *A Journey from London to Genoa through England, Portugal, Spain and France*, 4 vols (1770).

BARNARD, J. *Some Thoughts on the Scarcity of Silver Coin* (1759).

BEAWES, W. *Lex Mercatoria Rediviva: or the Merchant's Directory*, 2nd ed. (1761).

[BROMLEY, W.] *Several Years Travels through Portugal, Spain and Italy . . . Performed by a Gentleman* (1702).

CARY, J. *A Discourse on Trade* (1745).

An Essay towards Regulating the Trade . . . of this Kingdom, 2nd ed. (1719).

CASTAING, J. *Course of the Exchange* (1698 onwards).

COLBATCH, J. *Account of the Court of Portugal* (1700).

COSTIGAN, A. W. *Sketches of Society and Manners in Portugal*, 2 vols (1787).

CROFT, J. *Treatise on the Wines of Portugal* (York, 1788).

DALRYMPLE, W. *Travels through Spain and Portugal in 1774* (1777).

DECKER, M. *An Essay on the Causes of the Decline of the Foreign Trade* (1744).

DEFOE, D. *A General History of Trade* (1713).

The Trade with France, Italy, Spain and Portugal Considered (1713).

A Plan of the English Commerce (1728).

Mercator: or Commerce Retrieved (1713-14).

[EGLETON, J.] *A Vindication of the late House of Commons in Rejecting the Bill for Confirming the Eighth and Ninth Articles of the Treaty of Navigation and Commerce between England and France* (1714).

GEE, J. *The Trade and Navigation of Great Britain Considered*, 2nd ed. (1730).

HARRIS, J. *An Essay upon Money and Coins* (1757).

HAYNES, J. *Great Britain's Glory* (1715).

[JANSSEN, T.] *General Maxims in Trade* (1713).

KING, C. (ed.) *The British Merchant, or Commerce Preserv'd*, 3 vols (1721).

[MAGENS, N.] *The Universal Merchant* (1753).

Farther Explanations of some Particular Subjects contained in the Universal Merchant (1756).

PINTO, I. DE *An Essay on Circulation and Credit* (trans. by Rev. S. Baggs) (1744).

[POLLEXFEX, J.] *A Discourse of Trade, Coyn, and Paper Credit* (1697).

POSTLETHWAYT, M. *The Merchant's Public Counting House* (1750).

SAVARY, J. *Universal Dictionary of Trade and Commerce* (trans. from the French), 2nd ed., 2 vols (1757).

SMITH, J. *Chronicum Rusticum-Commerciale: or Memoirs of Wool*, 2 vols (1747).

SNELLING, T. *A View of the Silver Coin and Coinage of England* (1762).

A View of the Gold Coin and Coinage of England (1763).

A View of the Coins at this Time Current throughout Europe (1766).

TUCKER, J. *A Brief Essay on the Advantages and Disadvantages which respectively attend France and Great Britain with Regard to Trade* (1750).

UZTARIZ, G. DE *The Theory and Practice of Commercial Affairs* (trans. from the Spanish by J. Kippax), 2 vols (1751).

[WHATLEY, G.] *Reflections on Coin in General* (1762).

WHITWORTH, C. *State of the Trade of Great Britain* (1776).

WOOD, W. *A Survey of Trade* (1718).

Later Printed Works

BOOKS

ANONYMOUS, *The Story and Origin of Hunt, Roope & Company, London and Oporto* (1951).

ASHTON, T. S. *Economic Fluctuations in England, 1700-1800* (Oxford, 1959).
An Economic History of England: The 18th Century (1955).

AZEVEDO, J. LUCIO DE *Épocas de Portugal Economico*, 2nd ed. (Lisbon 1947).
O Marques de Pombal e a sua Época, 2nd ed. (Lisbon, 1922).

BALBI, A. *Essai Statistique sur le Royaume de Portugal et d'Algarve comparé aux autres États d'Europe* (Paris, 1822).

BOXER, C. R. *The Golden Age of Brazil, 1695-1750* (Berkeley, Los Angeles, 1962).

CALOGERAS, J. PANDIA *As Minas do Brasil e a sua Legislaçao:* 2 vols (Rio de Janeiro, 1904).

CARNAXIDE, V. DE *O Brasil na Administração Pombalina* (São Paulo, 1940).

CHEKE, M. *Dictator of Portugal* (1938).

CLAPHAM, J. *The Bank of England. A History*, 2 vols (Cambridge, 1944).

CLARK, G. N. *Guide to English Commercial Statistics, 1696-1782* (1938).

CRAIG, J. *The Mint: A History of the London Mint from A.D. 287 to 1948* (Cambridge, 1953).

DAVIS, R. *The Rise of the English Shipping Industry in the 17th and 18th Centuries* (1962).

DEANE, P. AND COLE, W. A. *British Economic Growth, 1688-1959* (Cambridge, 1962).

ERSKINE, D. (ed.) *Augustus Hervey's Journal* (1953).

ESTORNINHO, C. *O Terramoto de 1755 e a sua Repercussão nas Relaçoes Luso-Britânicas* (Lisbon, 1956).

FEAVEARYEAR, A. E. *The Pound Sterling* (Oxford, 1931).

FORRESTER, J. J. *Portugal and its Capabilities* (1860).

GODINHO, V. MAGALHÃES *Prix et Monnaies au Portugal, 1750-1850* (Paris, 1955).

GUEDES, A. MARQUES *A Aliança Inglêsa* (Lisbon, 1938).

HARING, C. H. *Trade and Navigation between Spain and the Indies in the Time of the Hapsburgs* (Cambridge, Mass., 1918).
The Spanish Empire in America (New York, 1947).

HEATON, H. *The Yorkshire Woollen and Worsted Industries* (Oxford, 1920).

HEMMEON, J. C. *The History of the British Post Office* (1912).

HERR, R. *The Eighteenth Century Revolution in Spain* (Princeton, 1958).

HILL, L. F. (ed.) *Brazil* (1947).

HOSKINS, W. G. *Industry, Trade and People in Exeter, 1688-1800* (Manchester, 1935).

HOTBLACK, K. *Chatham's Colonial Policy* (1917).

HOUBLON, LADY A. ARCHER *The Houblon Family* (1907).

INNIS, H. A. *The Cod Fisheries* (New Haven, 1940).

KENDRICK, T. D. *The Lisbon Earthquake* (1956).

LEVASSEUR, E. *Histoire du Commerce de la France* (Paris, 1911-12).

LIPSON, E. *The Economic History of England*, 3 vols (1915-31).

LIVERMORE, H. V. *A History of Portugal* (Cambridge, 1947).
(ed.) *Portugal and Brazil* (Oxford, 1953).

LOUNSBURY, R. G. *The British Fishery at Newfoundland, 1634-1763* (New Haven, 1934).

MACAULAY, R. *They Went to Portugal* (1946).

MCCULLOCH, J. R. *Old and Scarce Tracts on Money* (1856).

MACEDO, J. DE *A Situação Económica no Tempo de Pombal* (Oporto, 1951).
Problemas de História da Indústria Portuguesa no Século XVIII (Lisbon, 1963).

MCLACHLAN, J. O. *Trade and Peace with Old Spain, 1667-1750* (Cambridge, 1940).

MACPHERSON, D. *Annals of Commerce*, 4 vols (1805).

MAHAN, A. T. *The Influence of Sea Power upon History, 1600-1783* (1892).

MANCHESTER, A. K. *British Pre-Eminence in Brazil. Its Rise and Decline* (Chapel Hill, 1933).

MARSHALL, J. *A Digest of all the Accounts . . . of Great Britain and Ireland* (1833).

MAURO, F. *Le Portugal et l'Atlantique au XVIIe Siècle (1570-1670)* (Paris, 1960).

MORRELL, W. P. *The Gold Rushes* (1940).

NORMANO, J. F. *Brazil. A Study of Economic Types* (Chapel Hill, 1935).

OLIVEIRA, A. DE SALLES *Moedas do Brasil* (São Paulo, 1944).

OWEN, J. H. *War at Sea under Queen Anne, 1704-1708* (Cambridge, 1938).

PANTALEÃO, O. *A Penetração Comercial da Inglaterra na America Espanhola de 1713 a 1783* (São Paulo, 1946).

PARES, R. *War and Trade in the West Indies, 1739-63* (Oxford, 1936).
Yankees and Creoles. The Trade between North America and the West Indies before the American Revolution (1956).

PENSON, L. M. *The Colonial Background of British Foreign Policy* (1930).

PRADO, C. *História Economica do Brasil* (São Paulo, 1956).

RAU, V. *O Movimento da Barra do Douro durante o Século XVIII: uma Interpretação* (Oporto, 1958).

SELLERS, C. *Oporto, Old and New* (1899).

SHAW, W. A. *The History of Currency, 1252 to 1894* (n.d.).

(ed.) *Select Tracts and Documents illustrative of English Monetary History, 1626-1730* (1935).

SHILLINGTON, V. M. AND CHAPMAN, A. B. W. *The Commercial Relations of England and Portugal* (1907).

SIMON, A. L. *Bottlescrew Days* (1926).

The History of the Wine Trade in England, 3 vols (1909).

SIMONSEN, R. C. *Historia Economica do Brasil, 1500-1820*, 2 vols (São Paulo, 1937).

SMITH, J. *Memoirs of the Marquis de Pombal*, 2 vols (1843).

SOETBEER, A. *Edelmetall-Produktion und Werthverhältnis zwischen Gold und Silber* (Gotha, 1879).

SOMBRA, S. *Historia Monetaria do Brasil Colonial* (Rio de Janeiro, 1938).

SOUTHEY, R. *History of Brazil*, 3 vols (1810-19).

SUTHERLAND, L. S. *A London Merchant* (Oxford, 1933).

VAZ, J. FERRARO *Catálago das Moedas Portuguesas – Portugal Continental* (Lisbon, 1949).

WALFORD, A. R. *The British Factory in Lisbon* (Lisbon, 1940).

WARRE, J. *The Past, Present and Future State of the Wine Trade* (1823).

WESTERFIELD, R. B. *Middlemen in English Business* (New Haven, 1915).

WILLAN, T. S. *The English Coasting Trade, 1600-1750* (Manchester, 1938).

WILSON, C. H. *Anglo-Dutch Commerce in the Eighteenth Century* (Cambridge, 1941).

ARTICLES IN PERIODICALS

ALDEN, D. 'Manoel Luis Vieira: An Entrepreneur in Rio de Janeiro during Brazil's Eighteenth Century Agricultural Renaissance', *H.A.H.R.*, Vol. XXXIX (1959).

'The Population of Brazil in the Late Eighteenth Century: A Preliminary Survey', *H.A.H.R.*, Vol. XLIII (1963).

BROWN, V. L. 'Anglo-Spanish Relations in America in the Closing Years of the Colonial Era', *H.A.H.R.*, Vol. V (1922).

'The South Sea Company and Contraband Trade', *A.H.R.*, Vol. XXXI (1926).

'Contraband Trade: A Factor in the Decline of Spain's Empire in America', *H.A.H.R.*, Vol. VIII (1928).

'Anglo-French Rivalry for the Trade of the Spanish Peninsula, 1763-1783', *Smith College Studies in History*, Vol. XV (1929-30).

'Relations of Spain and Portugal, 1763-1777', *Smith College Studies in History*, Vol. XV (1929-30).

BURLEY, K. H. 'A Note on a Labour Dispute in early Eighteenth-Century Colchester', *Bulletin of the Institute of Historical Research*, Vol. XXIX (1956).

CARDOZO, M. S. 'The Collection of the Fifths in Brazil, 1695-1709', *H.A.H.R.*, Vol. XX (1940).

'The Guerra dos Emboabas, Civil War in Minas Gerais, 1708-1709', *H.A.H.R.*, Vol. XXII (1942).

CHRISTELOW, A. 'French Interest in the Spanish Empire during the Ministry of the Duc de Choiseul, 1759-1771', *H.A.H.R.*, Vol. XX (1941).

'Contraband Trade between Jamaica and the Spanish Main, and the Free Port Act of 1766', *H.A.H.R.*, Vol. XXII (1942).

'Economic Background of the Anglo-Spanish War of 1762', *Journal of Modern History*, Vol. XVIII (1946).

'Great Britain and the Trades from Cadiz and Lisbon to Spanish America and Brazil, 1759-1783', *H.A.H.R.*, Vol. XXVII (1947).

CLARK, G. N. 'War Trade and Trade War 1701-13', *Ec.H.R.*, Vol. I (1928).

DAVIES, R. 'English Foreign Trade, 1660-1700', *Ec.H.R.*, 2nd series, Vol. VII (1954).

'English Foreign Trade, 1700-1774', *Ec.H.R.*, 2nd series, Vol. XV (1962).

DAVIS, K. G. 'Joint Stock Investment in the Later Seventeenth Century', *Ec.H.R.*, 2nd series, Vol. IV (1952).

DEANE, P. 'The Output of the British Woollen Industry in the Eighteenth Century', *J.Ec.H.*, Vol. XVII (1957).

DIÉGUES, M. JR. 'As Companhias Privilegiadas no Comércio Colonial', *Rev. de H.*, No. 3 (1950).

DILLEN, J. G. VAN 'Amsterdam Marché Mondial des Métaux Précieux au XVIIe et au XVIIIe Siècle', *Revue Historique*, Vol. CLII (1926).

FISHER, G. 'Early Days of the British "Factory" ', *Historical Association, Lisbon Branch, Report*, 1946-50.

GODINHO, V. MAGALHÃES. 'Le Portugal, les Flottes du Sucre et les Flottes de l'Or, 1670-1770', *Annales*, Vol. V (1950).

HARKNESS, D. A. E. 'The Opposition to the 8th and 9th Articles of the Commercial Treaty of Utrecht', *Scottish Historical Review*, Vol. XXI (1924).

HIPWELL, H. HALLAM 'The Portuguese East India Company, 1754-6', *Historical Association, Lisbon Branch, Report*, 1941.

JAYNE, R. G. 'The Garland Family', *Historical Association, Lisbon Branch, Report*, 1945.

LODGE, R. 'The English Factory at Lisbon. Some Chapters in its History', *Transactions of the Royal Historical Society*, 4th series, Vol. XVI (1933).

MACEDO, J. DE 'Portugal e a Económia "Pombalina". Temas e Hipóteses', *Rev. de H.*, Vol. XIX (1954).

NELSON, G. H. 'Contraband Trade under the Asiento, 1730-1739', *A.H.R.*, Vol. LI (1945).

NETTELS, C. 'England and the Spanish-American Trade, 1680-1715', *Journal of Modern History*, Vol. III (1931).

PRESTAGE, E. 'The Anglo-Portuguese Alliance', *Transactions of the Royal Historical Society*, 4th series, Vol. XVII (1934).

REES, J. F. 'The Phases of British Commercial Policy in the Eighteenth Century', *Economica*, Vol. XIV (1925).

WALFORD, A. R. 'The British Community in Lisbon, 1755. The Earthquake Census?', *Historical Association, Lisbon Branch, Report*, 1946-50.

WILSON, C. H. 'The Economic Decline of the Netherlands', *Ec.H.R.*, Vol. IX (1939).

UNPUBLISHED THESES

BURLEY, K. H. The Economic Development of Essex in the Later Seventeenth and Early Eighteenth Centuries. University of London Ph.D. thesis (1957).

EDWARDS, J. K. The Economic Development of Norwich, 1750-1850. University of Leeds Ph.D. thesis (1963).

MATHEWS, E. F. J. Economic History of Poole, 1750-1850. University of London Ph.D. thesis (1957).

TURNER, M. E. Anglo-Portuguese Relations and the War of the Spanish Succession. University of Oxford D.Phil. thesis (1952).

Index

For Product Safety Concerns and Information please contact our EU
representative GPSR@taylorandfrancis.com
Taylor & Francis Verlag GmbH, Kaufingerstraße 24, 80331 München, Germany

www.ingramcontent.com/pod-product-compliance
Lightning Source LLC
LaVergne TN
LVHW011131300926
849160LV00008B/607

* 9 7 8 1 1 3 8 8 6 5 0 0 6 *